GIRL'S GUIDE
to SURVIVAL

First published in 2015 by New Holland Publishers Pty Ltd
London • Sydney • Cape Town • Auckland

The Chandlery Unit 009 50 Westminster Bridge Road London SE1 7QY United Kingdom
1/66 Gibbes Street Chatswood NSW 2067 Australia
218 Lake Road Northcote Auckland New Zealand

www.newhollandpublishers.com

ISBN 9781742575681

Managing Director: Fiona Schultz
Publisher: Diane Ward
Editor: Simona Hill
Designer: Lorena Susak
Production Director: Olga Dementiev
Printer: Toppan Leefung Printing Ltd

10 9 8 7 6 5 4 3 2 1

Keep up with New Holland Publishers on Facebook
www.facebook.com/NewHollandPublishers

GIRL'S GUIDE to SURVIVAL

The Savvy Girl's Guide to Mastering Household Management

Sarah Johannsen

Acknowledgements

A SHOUT OUT TO THOSE WHO MADE ME STRONGER

I must thank my Grandmother for teaching me these secrets. For the days I sat with the hints and tips book as she sewed, ironed, cooked and cleaned. I only wish she was still here to see me passing those skills along. Beryl May, I hope you're watching from a cloud.

That brings me to all of my Ask Sarah readers. Thank you so much for your support through the years. I can't believe the nice community we share. You voted with your likes, comments and emails on my site. You guys told me what YOU needed to know and that really helped me with this book.

A little shout out to some of my ladies in the Australian Sewing Guild. To my Marion girls, thanks for the refinements and your sharp minds. Thanks to the Board (Shirley, Louise, Toni especially) for understanding my commitments and for your unending enthusiasm. To dear Anne, how I wish my arms reached all the way to you. You have been so kind and encouraging and you share my joys.

I cannot thank my all-star support crew enough! These special three people are always there for me but they really stepped up their game when I took on this book. Massive thanks to:

To my husband, who put up with a lack of decent dinners and all kinds of crazy!. I am so lucky that he loves me so much and supports my various projects even when they turn the house and our lives upside down! You are rock solid and give the best advice. Thank you for keeping me safe.

My Mum, who spent her precious holiday leave bouncing around ideas with me and sitting by my side as I clacked away at the laptop. She did my dishes and ran errands to free up my time. She snorted with laughter when I stumbled reading out loud, giggled inappropriately with me when it got hard and always had a champagne ready for the milestones. I would be lost without her by my side.

And my wonderful best friend, Jenine Brown, who answered my anxious phone calls and read and re read this book with saintly patience. She speaks fluent Sarah, even before coffee and is expert at understanding what I mean and helping me to articulate it. I thought we'd dealt with every possible scenario in these 20 years of friendship but I never imagined asking you to proofread my book! I promise I'll return the favour when you write your opus. All three of you know, that I could not do what I do without you by my side. Thank you for sharing my unfettered joy and believing that this Adelaide girl would make good. Thank you hardly seems enough. xxxx

P.S. Thank you to my furry companions: Mr Pyjamas, Dorris and Fang. Your calm peace soothed me, and your comic relief kept me entertained.

About the Author

I started my blog, 'Ask Sarah', back in 2010. At the time, I was sharing recipes, tips and cleaning methods online, all the time. More and more often, random people contacted me with questions. Typing and retyping these snippets got tiring, so I started the blog to keep track of them all. I had no idea then that it would be a new career.

You might wonder how I came to know these things and why I am sharing them. I was an odd sort of child, obsessed with Martha Gardener's *Big Book of Hints and Tips*. My dear Mum was working full time, studying full time at uni and raising me solo. I got to spend lots of time with my Grandparents, especially my Grandma. She had lived through the war, nursing the whole time, and had a make-do-and-mend mentality. She was a curiosity to me with her hair in rollers, dressed in a housecoat and slippers at breakfast. Grandma shared cleaning wisdom from a time before anti-bacterial everything, where all you needed was a piece of soap, some bicarbonate of soda and white vinegar. I have such fond memories of collecting lemons and passion fruits from the garden and turning them into cordial, curd and cakes with her.

Then when I started the practical business of learning household management, I started out pressing hankies and got to move on to bigger items, such as shirts and dresses.

I marvelled at the button tin while Grandma altered clothes at the sewing machine.

When I hit 18, I moved into a rented place with housemates and the real learning curve began! Suddenly I had to budget, cook proper meals and clean things all by myself. At times I did tasks poorly and at times I had it all together. I made many mistakes. I moved a lot, managing 13 rental places in 12 years. There was cohesion and chaos but eventually in my late 20s, I rented a place by myself and stayed there for five years; just me and my frisky felines. After many years of temporary office work in all sorts of industries, I settled into a finance job. I cooked a lot, I cleaned a lot and I finally got the hang of a budget – better late than never, right?

But life sometimes throws a curve ball. I put down a deposit on my own flat and a few short weeks later met my husband. I decided I didn't want to be part of the corporate machine and started a course that would qualify me to teach the community about money management and assist people in financial hardship. Then Ask Sarah took off and I decided to write full time.

It was natural that at some point, I would put this information together in book format.

I understand that the internet holds so many answers but sometimes you just don't quite know the question. I've included all the things I wished that I knew earlier. It certainly would have made life easier! I have lovely friends who were in the same situations as me throughout their 20s but now have teenage children. They are only realising now, that they could have better prepared their offspring for running a household. Many of the questions I have answered on Ask Sarah seem so simple to me but the person asking needed to know. I was surprised to hear some questions repeatedly. More surprising was that people stated that they weren't sure what to search for to find the help they needed. Maybe you'll find some answers to questions you have in your mind, or simply find a new way to do something. Even better, it may save you some time and hassle! Or save you from a costly repair or replacement, or help get that stain out of your fave top.

Before you read the advice on these pages, know that I have tested each and every strategy I've suggested. I've learned from both my brilliant wins and tragic mistakes! So, I bring you the *Girl's Guide to Survival* – don't leave home without it!

Thank you for reading. Sarah xxx

Contents

Introduction 11

Make Your Home Your Own 13

    Decorating 14

    Moveable Storage 18

    Let There Be Light 20

    Hiding Ugly Things 22

Making It In the Bedroom and the Bathroom 25

    Laundry and Household Linens 26

Wardrobe and Personal Grooming Fixes 33

    Fixing Your Fashion 34

    Styling Safe and Cosmetic Cleans 46

Championing the Household Chores 53

    Appliance Maintenance 54

    Spring Cleaning and Landlord Inspections 59

Catering Know-How 70

    Keeping Cool in the Kitchen 72

    Kitchen Tools You Need to Own 76

Catering for Everybody 79

Five Recipes You Need to Know 81

Great Gatherings 91

Gifts, Birthdays and Occasions 94

Social Situations 99

Noisy Neighbours 100

Living Alone or With Roommates 103

Serious Stuff 107

Car Maintenance 108

Moving House and Changing Address 111

Things That Go Bump in the Night 117

Fixing Up Accidents and Incidents 120

Big Shopping and Budget Basics 124

A Final Word 128

Introduction

There is nothing like turning the key in your own front door! That first house has the biggest thrill but there is joy with every new home along the way. If this is your first move, it's probably a rental and you'll want to make it feel like your own. My first house smelled strongly of curry and I couldn't wait for it to smell like my cooking and cleaning and perfume. It had decaying curtains that were at least 30 years out of style and plenty of ugly features to match. It took me a while to decorate, clean and style it until it was a reflection of me. If you are starting out on your own for the first time, this is your chance to stamp your personality on your home and really make it your own. Even if you are a house-moving veteran, each new place presents different challenges and opportunities.

Make Your Home Your Own

Decorating

The thing about your décor is this – only you have to love it but everyone you invite into your home will see it. We dress and do our hair and makeup in a way that reflects who we are and we can change that day to day. Our home also reflects our personalities and even if you change things around regularly, it's much more static. Getting a handle on how to personalize your home is a subjective process. No two people will look at a space and decorate it the same. If you are a strong personality, you'll read what I have to say and be solidified in your ideas by the end. For the rest of you, I hope it provides some clues about how to make a space oh so you!

Purpose: You have to decide the function and purpose of a room before you decide on your décor. Does your lounge room also need to be a study space? Or does it need to be a filming space for YouTube? Does your bedroom need to double as a storage space for linens and other things? Does your dining room table get used for crafting, sewing or painting? Knowing how a space will be used is the first step in planning your design. If your space is doing double duty, getting the right furniture in first is key, then you can design the décor around it.

Functionality or Form vs Function: Once you know the purpose of a space you can work out how to accommodate the things you need to do in that space. Transformational furniture (such as a coffee table that can be changed into a proper dining table) can help a space look smooth and assist you to multi task. Small spaces may benefit from storage couches, and coffee tables that become dining tables. Foldaway furniture isn't always about small spaces either – think adjustable or leaved tables, fold-up tables and chairs, fold-out couches and specialty items such as sewing cabinets. Then there is sneaky storage, such as a small chest of drawers used instead of a decorative table. Many retailers have attractive storage solutions that look great and are budget friendly.

Comfort and Ease of Use: There is no point having a couch that folds out or creates storage or turns into a small water vehicle if it isn't comfortable. Let's face it, if it isn't comfy or it's hard to use, you'll probably ignore it. There's also no point in having to crane your neck while you sit on it in order to watch TV. Make sure you'll really use and enjoy what you buy.

Block It Out: Once you've figured out what furniture you need, how it will be used and that it's comfortable, you need to be sure you've got space to fit it in the room. Start by positioning your biggest item. If you don't want to play a real, live game of Tetris, grab a measuring tape and plot it on paper or using one of the many free room-designing apps. We recently renovated and my tech- savvy husband made full 3D video renders to help me plan things. It's not just a question of 'will it fit', it's also 'will that work for me'.

LET THE FUN BEGIN

There is no magic décor formula, but I do have a few theories that help me out. Getting all excited about pattern and colour and texture is the best element of decorating! In the past I've gone to some crazy effort to get the look right. In my first place, there was a space where a dining room table should rightly go but I didn't have a table. And my decorator budget could be measured in coins! Three blocks away, there were a few things marked as free after a garage sale. I rolled a round, crappy dining room table of chipped laminate home those three blocks. Then I went back for the two ancient chrome and orange vinyl chairs. The backs of the seats were in perfect nick but the seats were cracked and broken. Not to be dissuaded, I picked up an orange and teal duvet cover set for next to nothing in the supermarket. I unscrewed the chair seats and used a staple gun to cover them with the pillow cases and used the duvet cover as a table cloth. Maybe you think that sounds awful and ghetto but I was 18 and broke and at the time it made me so very, very happy. And it proves a point about everyone's tastes being different.

That house was the first opportunity I had to impose my taste on a space. I made the dodgiest set of curtains with swathes of home-dyed calico and clumsy hand stitching, I arranged magazines over the mark on the coffee table and fixed chips in the paint with nail polish. I've had all sort of décor: beige, white and sophisticated, neon, candy and fun, and now a blend of the '50s and '60s meets minimal modern.

This is your house. Hear that again, this is your house. And you should have what makes you happy. Don't be constrained! Our homes are places of sanctuary. Your idea of sanctuary is different to mine. I've always had a rebellious streak when it comes to décor. I've had shocking and black and white nudes on my walls, collections of all types displayed, and most recently a renewed vigour when it comes to eye-popping colour. There are so many places where we can't be quite ourselves, so our home should be the quiet and gentle expression or total riot of who we are. Don't bother trying to please others (unless they live there too). Let it be you! Not what is current or fash or right now. Not something that you hope other people will like. This is the time to shine baby! I will say that there are NO rules but if the path isn't clear, think about these things:

Colour: Maybe you have a desired colour scheme or maybe it is to be determined by big furniture, carpets or walls. Either way, you've got a colour in mind, right? We will call it the core colour. There are three ways to play it – match, contrast, complement. Either way the other colours you choose to use alongside it will be called your colour palette. The following rules work for everything, outfits, makeup, room design. Grab your colour wheel, I prefer the kind that has many segments.

Match: Pick the tones to each side of your core colour. These colours and tones will be the ones you use to make your room.

Contrast: Find the opposite of your core colour and use it to accent.

Complement: Find the opposite of your core colour, look to the colours at each side of the opposite. These will be your accents.

You'll also need some neutral in the mix – white, black, browns, gold, silver as well as our other neutral friends such as beige and grey. Note, sometimes a neutral can be part of your colour palette and sometimes a colour can be a neutral.

I'll explain what I mean by using my real life lounge room as an example. In it, there are cupboards and a TV on a wall. They're black, white and red. That red is not a true red though, more of a raspberry. My couch is red but more of a strawberry red and my floor is a warm wood. So far we have two reds, black, white and brown. So, it's all neutral except for the reds. Opposite red on the colourwheel is green. But I was working some advanced complement. Which means I am using the direct opposite, green and the colours at each side of green which are teal blues and yellow greens. I have teals, greens and yellows in my rug and throw cushions. It's a lovely discordant harmony. But then I needed a throw so I can keep warm on TV nights. I added a hot magenta pink, bright teal and grey this way. It doesn't look discordant because these colours form a complex harmony and in this room, red is the neutral. It's a unifying force because it is still the most dominant colour.

My friends are crazy minimalists! White walls, beige tile, grey carpet. Their furniture is unremarkable. Grey couch, black table, white bookcase. They have a lot of art and want to show it off. But they still have objects just for decoration, ornaments such as candlesticks and vases and almost all are silver or black. Silver has stepped out of neutral to become a part of the colour palette. Instead of blending in, it becomes the accent.

Sometimes it's impossible to change the colour structure of a room (*see* Hiding Ugly Things) but you can always add your flair! Pictures, throw cushions, throw blankets and your own 'dust collectors' can make all the difference.

The Rule of Three: Match, contrast, and complement – you need them in a room scheme. This is the secret to having it look just right. Three is the answer! Three colours, three patterns, three style elements. Groups of three are visually pleasing, memorable and effective.

If you are adding a pop of colour, repeat it three times for a cohesive look. If you are combining prints, use three patterns together. Group objects in threes, such as three vases, or three pictures.

Dust Collectors, Tchotchkes and Tat: Whatever vernacular you use to describe it, this is the stuff you have on surfaces. Maybe you have been collecting something from childhood or you just like stuff and buy it, you'll have…things. Displaying them artfully is a process. I like to start with a fresh room, clear surfaces and add one by one. If you have a lot of this sort of stuff, do you want all of it on show at once? One of my fave ways to keep things fresh is to rotate my stuff. Don't cover every space unless you really want to. My chosen home is tiny. I have to make choices. My husband isn't in love with my flamingo, crochet plants, flying ducks and matryoshka collection. But he is happy for me to have it. But my next buy means a retirement for one of them.

Make things look less weird or crazy by grouping them. Not just like with like but colour, shape, era or style. And if you have a massive collection of books, ceramic bears, cameras, grouping nicely can be the win. Consider arranging books by alphabet, subject or spine colour. Don't just sprinkle your home, make it a design, make it thematic. This kind of harmony will put others at ease.

MAKE THE MOST OF YOUR WALLS

If you rent, you may be limited when it comes to making holes in the walls and hanging artwork. Always get approval from the landlord before putting a screw or nail in the wall; you don't want the cost of the repair to come out of your deposit! If you can't hang artwork exactly where you want it, you'll have to get creative.

Picture Rail Hooks: If you live in an older house with a picture rail, grab some picture rail hooks. You can hang things directly from the hook itself or use fishing line to hang things lower.

Command Products: These stick-on hooks come in all sorts of styles and claim to be damage free. I have used them with great success but be careful when removing them and go very slowly to avoid damage. It's also worth noting that they may come away from the wall in extreme heat.

Reusable Adhesive and Poster Putty: This can be a perfect solution for lightweight objects. I have had issues with these types of products leaving a mark and they can fail in extreme heat and cold.

Fishing Line: If a hook is positioned too high or you would like to hang a second picture below the first, fishing line is the answer. Just make sure it is of a heavy enough gauge to support the weight of the picture.

Moveable Storage

Somehow, no matter how small or how expansive your living space, there is never enough storage. It's a universal truth! I swear I've found every sneaky storage space in my years of small-space living. It can be hard to think outside the box, especially if you can't attach things to the walls but these ideas should expand your world...

Look Up: If you don't have much floor space, think about tall shelving or bookcases that utilize the vertical space. If you are able to hang shelves, you could put them around the room, high up. Boxes, tubs and baskets on top of cupboards or even the refrigerator can boost storage space. Just make sure you have a step ladder to add and remove items from up high!

Bin It: Use tubs, bins or freestanding shelves to get the most out of cupboards. Group like items into tubs or bins that go back the full depth of the cupboard, then you can pull it out like a drawer. Items at the back are easily accessible and less likely to be forgotten. Plus it keeps things tidy and organized.

Get Clear: Grab some clear acrylic makeup organizers to store and organize small items. They are fabulous at making the best of small bathroom or cupboards and look great on counters. They are perfect bedside table caddies for skincare, jewelry and accessories, or even craft or office supplies.

Hide It: Don't forget the space under your bed or couch, you can get tubs on wheels designed to fit in these spaces.

Screen It: Use screens to hide areas of ugly storage such as clothes racks or stacked boxes.

Chop It: Chopping blocks on wheels are a great way to expand bench space, while items can be stored below. You can even get quite small ones that would fit in almost any kitchen!

CLUTTER HOT SPOTS

Hallways, entryways, coffee and dining room tables seem to naturally attract clutter! Having designated spaces for things makes everything look more streamlined and makes putting things away easier.

Quick Tips to Keep Clutter at Bay

File It: I keep a letter rack near the door to stop all those catalogues I want to read, mail I have to attend to and bills I have to pay from cluttering my coffee table or kitchen bench. I found this really did stop things from being left around the house because it is RIGHT by the door. If you have an entry way with a small table or cupboard then you could make that furniture your mail stop. And it doesn't have to be a letter rack it could be a decorative storage box or even a pretty tote on a hook if space is tight.

Find It: Have a place for keys. A wall-mounted key rack, a decorative bowl or conveniently located drawer, are all good choices. Depending on the option you choose you can also store wallets here too.

Keep It: Make a spot for your handbag, shoes, coat and umbrella. Even in the tiniest apartment there is room for a little table/bookshelf/chair where you can put your bag and shoes when you arrive home. It will help keep your day-to-day stuff organized and make for a quick getaway in the morning.

Corral It: If you like to keep things (like lip balm, moisturiser or a pen and paper) where you sit, consider a decorative box or basket for these items to live in. Many things can be visual clutter; one attractive item looks streamlined.

Push It − Real Good: If you are like me, everything has a remote − the stereo, the TV, the heater. And they always look messy. Store them in a larger size pencil cup from the local office supply or make a cute one from attractive jars or tins.

Let There Be Light

There is more to lighting than screwing in a bulb! Mood lighting isn't just decorator phraseology. The lighting that you choose can set the mood of a room. Getting it right will help you cook dinner without chopping your finger, help you read a book easily, take a more flattering selfie or Skype, or make people feel comfortable in your home. Before we get too far in let's consider the bulb you choose.

Fixtures and Fittings: Aren't they all the same? Fittings vary from country to country but the most common types you will come across are Edison (sometimes called screw bulbs) which have an obvious screw pattern on the metal part, or Bayonet-style globes, which have a smooth metal part with two pins. If you have down lights (those small ones that are most often flush with the ceiling) they also have at least two variations, small pins that are the same width throughout their length or pins with a circular disk at their end. Size does matter here! If you are unsure which globe to get, take the existing globe (or whole lamp!) to a lighting store and ask. They will tell you exactly the fitting you need.

Right Light: Regardless of your fitting, there is a dizzying array of choices – energy saving, halogen, LED and retro filament bulbs! Before you choose, think about the activity, and the purpose of a room. For example; I have a very bright, cold/white, fluorescent energy-saving bulb as my main kitchen light. It's perfect for seeing what I'm doing. This is about bright, task lighting. I also have low, pendulum lighting over my kitchen bench that has rich golden halogen bulbs. When I have guests, it is flattering, soft and just enough for me to finish my dishes. My lounge has flattering halogen down lights and lamps with soft, golden, filament globes. Think about how you use each space, and the kinds of light you wish each to have. If you are constrained to the lighting you have, don't fret because…

A Little Twinkle In the Eyes: Lighting can create a mood with such little effort! You have your overhead lighting sorted but don't forget the lamps! I think the best lighting schemes have down light (your overhead), up light (lamps, lighting strings) and ambient mid light. Think about your favourite romantic movie… they used all of these tricks, even if you didn't see them! Lamps are cheap and if you are on budget, LED lamps are very cheap to run! They will cast a blueish light that can be less than face flattering but when it comes to task lighting, they can't be beat! But don't discount cheap and effective glowy lighting! Clear Christmas lights are so pretty and effective.

Making the Mood: So we have established the idea of great lighting! But how to get that great selfie, or put your friends at ease from the second they come in to your home. Have lots of light, different kinds and literally glow! When choosing a house, natural light should be on your mind but if you are like me, maybe that wasn't a first thought! Bright, task lighting will show makeup colours best but a more yellow light will assist in softening features. People feel welcomed into a bright, well lit home but turn off the task lights and use all your lamps and soft lighting to make them comfortable.

Hiding Ugly Things

Let's face it, not every house is a perfect paradise. The perfect house may come with flaws that, as a renter, you have no power to change. And we have all moved into that perfect house and realized it has almost no power points and the ones it has are in all the wrong places. Ugly carpets, ugly walls, ugly bathrooms. They happen and there are certainly ways to fix them! Or hide them or just make less of them. Whether you are in brown hell, a '70s wallpaper haze or have to run cords across the universe, this chapter has you covered!

Less Than Magical Carpets: So your carpet is gross. Maybe it is universally disgusting or maybe it has patches of ick. Or maybe it's some sort of lino that doesn't have illusions of comfort at all. Not all of the solutions offered below will work to minimise their effect but each may work for this or that. You'll know the look you are going for and the purpose you are aiming at. That said, you may need to be flexible if the flooring really peeves you! My best advice is to be directed by your plan but remain flexible!

- Simple, cheap rugs can cover an ugly area of carpet or the worst bits.
- If you want the look of new carpet on the cheap, measure the space and make a scale drawing. A remnant carpet sales place could make a rug that custom fits the whole room.
- Carpet tiles or sea grass matting can be an inexpensive way to 'over pave' a room.
- Consider a room with throw cushions on the floor.
- Arrange furniture, plants, stacks of books or decorative objects over icky stains or marks.
- Use your lighting.
- Cut down the legs of a dining room table to make a large coffee table. It covers floor area and is perfect for low level dining.
- You can also have carpets professionally cleaned or *see* upholstery cleaning.

Cords, Pipes and Such Like
- Attach a skirt or curtain around the bottom of furniture or sinks to hide cords or pipes.
- An artful stack of books under a table can hide the cord of a table lamp, cords or a router.
- Hide a router and phone chargers in an attractive storage box. Just cut a hole in the back for the cords.
- Use decorative cord clips to travel cords around a room.

Walls To Watch

- Use a curtain to hide an ugly wall.
- Use a lightweight canvas artwork over a wall mounted TV to disguise it.
- Removable wallpaper or removable decals can add interest to your walls or even your appliances.
- Position lighting.

The Master of Disguise

Regardless of your 'ugly' issues, keep clean lines and thematic threads in your décor. If your house is strongly themed and your taste and preferences are clearly evident it will guide people to the joy, fun and even simplicity of your taste and your home. Making your house your own is about creating an illusion that everything may not be perfect but is you and to your taste, even if you are hiding a stained carpet. They won't notice the stained carpet in a sea full of you and your fine tastes. Nothing says clean and organised like a clean surface. If you are living in cramped quarters, a clear (even tiny) space will have impact. Clear spaces will keep people thinking your space is larger and nicer than it seems even if there is clutter due to storage issues. Keeping things tidy will distract from the odd stain or discordant flooring issue. When visitors enter your house they will not be taking in everything, but they will notice interesting items, clean clear lines and themes. Distraction is everything, even in the perfect house. You know what you want people to see and understand about you when they walk through the front door. Streams of colour coordination, artfully placed items and mood lighting will tell people what you want them to know about you. Importantly, if it pleases you then that is all that matters. When you walk through your front door think about what you enjoy about your home and how you can make that evident to others.

Making It In the Bedroom and the Bathroom

Laundry and Household Linens

It's worth getting to know which products to use for everyday freshness and emergency stain treatments. There are so many laundry products out there, how do you choose? Most of your choice comes down to personal preference and not much else but here's a quick overview.

A BUYER'S GUIDE TO TOWELS, SHEETS AND QUILTS

No one likes a scratchy or bald towel, or pilled sheets, or flat pillows, or a quilt that leaves them shivering at night. Understanding the language used to differentiate the options makes it much easier to get the right product for you in a sea of purchasing opportunities.

Bed linen and towels seem so simple and elementary and most of those items are just... there. I know that functional seems boring and a discussion on linens probably reminds you of your Gran. And being reminded of your Gran isn't far off it. There once was a time when a young woman had a glory chest. Women in her family would contribute the things of everyday life, such as linens and blankets to her glory chest so that when she married and moved away from home she would have the beginnings of her household. Good quality things, things that would last until the couple was established. But these days you're lucky to take off with the stuff you had when you were living at home! And these choices matter. You want your bedroom to be a place you can relax in, be comfortable in and enjoy. And if you're me, you want it to be Pinterest and Instagram worthy too.

I've made my share of mistakes; ugly blue towels as well as cheap towels that absorbed nothing, and polyester blend sheets with such bad pilling that they gave my legs what looked like razor burn. When I first moved out, I put a set of Egyptian cotton towels on layby. I dutifully paid them off and was so excited about how long my towels would last! Last they did but the very fashionable cornflower blue soon became the very out-dated cornflower blue. Eventually I could stand them no more and used them for dyeing my hair. I learned quickly that when you are buying for keeps, the boring white (or black for that matter) will stand a thousand fashion trends. As you'll read below, I stick to quality basics and I follow trends with cheaper pieces. Investing in the good stuff means it will be years before you need a replacement, freeing up cash for fabulous, frivolous, fashion pieces that you can change on whim.

Luxurious fabrics and spa soft towels can be yours, even on a budget; it's all about shopping smart. Read this guide and get acquainted with the terms used to describe and measure what you're buying. Go to high-end shops and get touchy feely with the things on offer, ask well informed questions. Once you know what you're after, check prices, online resources, hit outlet stores and never forget good old layby. As a wise woman once said to me – "Good sheets and towels are like a kiss on the skin. The world could go to hell but at least I am wrapped in kisses."

Towels

There are a few things to consider when buying towels. A good quality set could last you 10 years! But a cheap, poor quality set might not last the year. I strongly suggest buying the best quality you can. Not only will it last longer but it will absorb more and probably feel more luxurious. We all know fashions change (and who knows what your next bathroom will look like!) so if you invest in quality, consider going for all white or all black towels. Makeup and hair dye should bleach out of white towels though frequent bleaching will break down the fibres over time. Makeup and hair dye stains won't show on black but you may find a fine layer of towel fluff in your bathroom.

I'd recommend you buy towels that are 100 percent cotton. Cotton is very absorbent, sucking up almost 25 times its weight. Look for densely packed little loops in the pile, if you can see the base fabric easily, it won't be as absorbent. A good quality towel will feel heavier than it looks.

Don't be confused by the type of cotton. The longer the cotton fibre, the stronger and more absorbent the towel will be. Not every towel will display the cotton type on the label, package or ticket price but it's nice to be informed when you are shopping.

Combed: Combed means that the shorter fibres are removed, which keeps the towel strong and helps guard against pilling.

Egyptian Cotton: Made of extra-long threads, Egyptian cotton is often considered to be the most luxurious.

Pima or Supima Cotton: Pima cotton has extra-long staple fibers that are both strong and absorbent.

Turkish Cotton: Features an extra-long staple and has great absorbency and durability.
You will also see a towel measured in GSM (Grams per Square Meter).
300–400 GSM is considered a light towel. Think hand towels, dish towels.
400–600 GSM is considered a medium towel. Think beach towels, budget towels.
600–900 GSM is considered a heavy towel. Think luxurious bath towel.

Laundry Tips
- Wash new towels before using to remove any 'softeners' added in manufacture and to set the colours.
- Do not use fabric softener with towels or sheets, just add a cup of white vinegar to the wash

instead. Fabric softener can reduce the towel's absorbency and the breathability of sheets.
- Don't wash or dry clothes with towels. Your clothes will come out covered in towel fluff.

So, maybe you can't afford great towels right now. If you buy some cheapies to see you through while you save for some luxury ones, don't chuck them when they are replaced! Here are some great uses for old towels:
- Use them when doing a home hair dye.
- Protect your floor when using home leg waxes.
- Use them when cleaning your hair or make up brushes.
- Cut one into squares and use them to wipe off make up brushes when you are getting ready.
- Cut one up and use it to clean stuff.
- Sit on it while applying false tan.

Sheets and Covers

Sheets are another one of those things you don't want to skimp on – pilled or scratchy sheets are no fun! I like to splurge on high quality white sheets (fitted bottom and flat top sheets) that will last for years and go with everything. White can be bleached to remove hair dye and false tan incidents but regular bleaching will shorten the lifespan. Then I buy cheaper, fashionable quilt covers, which are more budget friendly. If you use a top sheet, the quality of the quilt cover is less important because it doesn't really touch your skin. I want to replace my quilt cover when the trend is over, or it gets stained. Let's face it, I sometimes work from bed, paint my nails on it, eat a quick snack over it – you get the idea! You may go for one classic, expensive, quality quilt cover that will last (and have the option to use it with or without a top sheet). So before you go shopping think about what will suit you.

Sheets are generally 100 percent cotton (my choice) or a cotton polyester blend. Pure cotton will breathe better and generally feel softer. Egyptian cotton is considered the most luxurious of cottons. Polyester blends tend to wrinkle less but can yellow if bleached. You may also come across linen sheets. Linen is very breathable and cooling but wrinkles very easily and is very expensive. Less expensive linen can be quite rough and scratchy. In the colder months you may go for flannel/flannelette sheets, which have a fluffy, brushed texture and can be made of cotton, wool, synthetics or a blend. There are plenty of other words on the packet that might confuse you. These generally refer to the way the fabric was woven and the characteristics the weave creates.

Poplin: A tightly woven fabric, often on the lighter side.

Percale: Tightly woven, medium weight and feels crisp and cool.

Sateen: Has an elaborate weave that make it feel soft and creates a soft sheen.

Jacquard: A specially loomed fabric in which the design is woven into the fabric.

You will also see bed linen labelled by thread count (TC). This refers to how many threads are in a square inch.

- 200 or less: Budget sheets, likely to be a bit scratchy.
- 300–400: Mid range, less expensive.
- 400–800: High end, soft sheets.
- 900 or more: Luxurious, expensive, soft. Sheets in this range (particularly sateens) can become a bit thick and stiff and therefore less breathable.

Quilts, Doonas or Duvets

The kind of quilt that is best for you depends on the temperature of where you live, how warm you like to be in bed, if you are prone to allergies, whether you change your quilt with the seasons or have the same one year round, and of course, your budget. You might like your quilt to feel lighter than air or you may prefer a quilt with a little weight; it's a personal choice. I love the warmth and weight of wool quilts and I always buy a quilt bigger than my bed (that is a king-size quilt on a queen-size bed). Having a bit more quilt feels plush, makes the bed look nice and avoids night-time tug of war! A good quilt can be pricey but could potentially last for years. You really want to be happy with what you buy so make sure you go and check some quilts out in store before deciding. Once you know what you want, hunt the sales, check out outlet stores and check prices online and don't forget about layby. Don't be fooled by super cheap $20 quilts in supermarkets and variety stores. I find these go lumpy and horrible in a couple of weeks! That said they are okay to get you through, or for a mate crashing on the couch.

Quilts with natural fillings are soft, light and comfortable and allow your skin to breathe. They are also highly resilient and tend to last longer than those with synthetic fillings. However, synthetics can be washed at home so this might be a practical choice if you suffer from allergies, or if your quilt is likely to require frequent laundering. The main quilt filling choices are:

Feather and Down: This is made up of a feathers that create poof and the down, soft feathers with a soft flexible quill. Feather quilts generally feel very light and fluffy. The down traps body warmth, the higher the percentage of down, the softer, warmer and fluffier the quilt will be. These quilts are measured by the percentage of down to feathers. Both goose and duck feathers and down can be found on the market. Both are great but the bigger the bird and the colder the climate it lives in, the warmer it will be.

Wool: Wool fibres trap body heat so are very warm in winter. Wool also wicks moisture and perspiration in the warmer weather. Wool can feel heavier than feather and down quilts. Such quilts are measured in grams per square metre (GSM), the higher the GSM, the warmer the quilt will be.

Cotton: Is a cooler, lighter weight choice. It is moisture absorbent so is good for summer, warmer climates or for those who prefer a lightweight quilt. Cotton quilts are also measured in GSM, the higher the GSM; the warmer the quilt will be.

Synthetic: Synthetic covers a wide range of materials but many synthetic quilts are polyester or microfiber. Synthetics feel light and fluffy and are generally the cheapest option. Synthetic quilts are also measured in GSM, the higher the GSM, the warmer the quilt will be. The advantage of synthetic quilts is that they can be washed, either in a home washing machine or at the Laundromat.

Handy Washing and Drying Hints

The best way to keep your quilt fresh is to frequently air it, whether that is on a clothes line or on a balcony or veranda. This will help eliminate odour, dry perspiration and kill dust mites.

If you are drying sheets inside, two dining chairs placed the right distance apart will create a make shift clothes line. Just place the sheet over the backs of the chairs. Of course, this will wet (and possibly mark) upholstered chairs. Keep that in mind when deciding if that is an option.

Adding 1 cup (250 ml/8 fl oz) of white vinegar to the wash when washing towels will help keep them fluffy when line dried or dried on a clothes arier.

If you are in a two-storey home, can you hang sheets over the bannister? Of course, you are putting a wet item on the surface of the bannister rail and this may damage paintwork etc. And unpainted metal may put rust on your sheets. Weigh the options and think about possible damage before you give it a go.

Pillows

Unlike the other items here, buying higher quality or more expensive doesn't necessarily mean better. Pillows are uber personal. How high you like your pillow (the loft), the fibre content, the shape…it all depends on how you sleep. And, how many pillows is personal, too. Personally, I like a bed with lots of pillows. It looks pretty when the bed is made and is excellent for TV watching. Some of my pillows come off at night to create a perfect sleep space. See, some of you just read that and thought 'OMG how fussy'. It's personal, alright? Most beds these days have a European pillow at the back and two standard pillows at the front. More or less, as you please. I also highly recommend body pillows. They are long pillows that run the length of the bed and they are perfect for curling up with. Body pillows are awesome to hug but they are great if you have back, hip or knee pain and they can be great as a behind-your-head pillow that runs the length of the headboard. Of course, you can add all sorts of decorative pillows too. The types of pillows that you are likely to find are:

Latex: Resilient and long lasting. Can be particularly beneficial for people who suffer from allergies. Of course, they're not good for those with latex sensitivities or allergies.

Synthetic: Synthetic pillows are easy to care for as they can be washed in a large capacity washing machine. They are ideal for anyone sensitive to, or allergic to, natural fillings, and are light in weight.

Feather and Down: Very soft, fluffy and light. These pillows feel dreamy but won't give too much support behind your back if you are sitting up in bed.

Wool: Dense, soft and has excellent moisture wicking, perfect for sweaty sleepers.

Memory Foam: Forms around you but has great support and longevity.

Many pillows these days are labelled with a sleeping position such as 'side sleeper' or 'back sleeper'. The thing with pillows is, get out there and touch them! I have a European pillow, then three standard pillows on each side of my bed. I bought three different kinds of standard pillow and labelled them. I road tested each for a month and when I found a clear winner I made a note of it. When replacement time came, I knew which ones to buy! Simple.

Bedrooms should be our sanctuary from the world. They offer a place of rest and repose and are a comfort when the world is hard. No matter how gorgeously decorated, no matter the luxury of the linens, our bedrooms are often where we watch TV, film video, work, eat and manicure. It's okay; I do it too. My bedroom has my laptop, my phone charger, my TV, my printer and an Ikea over-the-bed table where I often eat dinner. And yeah, I filmed a youTube film clip there once. But with all of that, remember that it is your bedroom, your sanctuary. I keep a fancy room spray (I had candles till a cat singed its tail) and my nicer skincare products there and I make sure I use them. I have both task and ambient lighting and blinds with curtains for keeping the world outside. Make your bedroom your place of luxury. Have a quilt that makes you feel like you are in a cloud, soft sheets to slide into after a candlelit bath and snuggly soft towels that feel like silk. You deserve to be rubbed up the right way!

Wardrobe and Personal Grooming Fixes

Fixing Your Fashion

I'm not going to quote statistics about how many clothes we own and how little of them we wear. But getting dressed is less of a struggle when you can find what you need. Even better when the clothes you need are in good repair and neatly pressed. If that sounds like a dream, you can make it a reality, just read on.

CLEARING THE CLUTTER

Let me guess, you have too many clothes and nothing to wear? There are so many systems for closet clearing, all of them promising freedom from clutter. I think that how you react emotionally to your clothes, your personality type and how strongly your style is defined make all the difference to how you keep clothes. If you flounder over each outfit decision, maybe you are feeling insecure or maybe you haven't found your style yet. Your style is what makes you feel 'you' in what you wear. Once you find it, some decisions will come more easily. Of course, your style will change with time. It will be affected by your lifestyle and taste and the life roles you have: a corporate job, or having children, or being a fashion blogger. But, if something is your style right now, to you it will just feel right. Everyone has an outfit or two that puts them at ease and makes them feel 'them'. When you have a whole wardrobe of those outfits, getting dressed is easy.

There are so many emotional reasons behind a cluttered wardrobe. I think most people are hoarders or optimists. Both have an underlying emotional thread and that's why it's hard to clear the clutter! You could be one or the other, a bit of both or feel like none of it is 'you'. Both the optimist and the hoarder have trouble refining and reducing their wardrobe clutter. The whole aim is to have a wardrobe full of things you love to wear, that is free from the junk you don't wear. I have some tips to help you get there.

THE BODY AND STYLE OPTIMIST

If you are in the habit of buying things that don't quite fit or aren't really you now but perfect for the you that you'd like to be, Optimism could be your problem!

Orphans: My friend has a ton of what we call orphaned items. They fit, she likes them but they don't seem to go with anything and thus, they don't get worn. To help solve this problem I encouraged her to wear new items immediately after purchase. That helps her find items that match while she is still super in love with her new find. Wearing an item straightaway helps you to see if it has any failings (it constantly falls off your shoulder, is too short without another layer, shrinks in the wash) and to fix any issue quickly, or work out if you can deal with the problem. It also imbeds the new item on your outfit planning memory so you don't forget you own the damn thing! Existing orphans must be matched and worn this way or you need to consider selling or donating them to someone else. The recipient may just have a perfect match!

Fit and Fix: If something plain doesn't fit, see my hoarder info below. But if it fits but doesn't fit well (pants too long, armhole gaping, shoulder strap too long) consider your love factor. Is it worth a trip to the alteration shop? Can it be worked round (cami under it, different bra, roll it up)? Be honest! If it's not 'you' or you wouldn't make those efforts, sell or donate it to someone else.

Reduce the Pain: You may have many items that still have their original store tags or are as new. Stop clocking the financial cost that you paid out for them and consider the emotional cost to you now. Keeping clothes that don't work just mocks you when you get dressed. No one wants to try on seven different outfits made of orphans and things that don't work. It makes you feel like your body is wrong, but really it's the clothes. Get rid of what doesn't work, new, old, cheap or costly. To lessen the blow and really make sure you're ready to part company, set out the things that should be rehomed where you can see and consider them. If, after a few days, you haven't found a way to give them new life, it's time for someone else to love them.

THE HOARDER

If you keep clothes because you wore them in high school or the day you got a great job or because one day you may lose 20 kg (44 lb) and think that one day you may fit into your favourite jeans that you've kept from 2001, or because it once belonged to your mum/gran/friend etc, you may be a Hoarder!

The Size Issue: I've had some significant weight gain but I'm sure I don't need jeans in every size from 8 to 22! Whether you've gained or lost, clothes that don't fit you will defeat you every time you get dressed. I've inadvertently worn too tight tops and pulled them down all day. To have anything more than 'this fits' and 'fat day' clothing is mental madness that will only hurt you. Try it on and if it's not your size let someone else love it. If you lose/gain you will not want the old thing. You will want something new. Stern self-talk here is required and nothing else will do. Employ an honest friend if you are too in love with things to see the obvious flaw – that they simply don't fit.

I Wore That When: OMG! With unlimited space you would keep everything! It's not a dress; it's a memory. But unless you want to die under boxes of dresses, you must limit what you keep! I allow 10 sentimental items that are not wearable. I also allow four occasion specific, wearable, sentimental garments. What I mean by that are items such as ball gowns and faux furs that fit and I would wear to a suitable occasion. If it's sentimental and wearable I must wear it at least three times in a year. Or it's gone. And that's it!

Reduce 'Selling or Donating' Pains: I've really learnt to get things out of my closet, but for years I used a special method to help me loosen my sentimental attachments to things I am not wearing and bless without tears or feeling bad. As you go through your wardrobe sort the things that won't be going back in the closet into three piles, unwearable by anyone, sell or donate (for the things that have had their day), suitcase (for things you can't quite bear to part with). Ditch the unwearable, give away or sell those items set aside and pack the rest into a suitcase. Store it as you will but I find it best to store it with a friend or family member so that I might help myself resist the urge to rummage. Keep the suitcase for six months to a year, no longer. If you have been able to leave it, forget it and not rummage, have someone take the contents and sell or donate them to someone else. Since you've lived without its contents, not needed them and still retained the memories without the aid of those garments, now's the time to let someone else love them.

ON SELLING AND DONATING

My friend has changed her thinking about donating items of unwanted clothing so now when she gives away clothes, she thinks of it not as gifting the recipient but that instead she is giving herself a gift. Anything earmarked for donation was bought with love and optimism but as it leaves her hands my friend scrutinizes why it didn't work. That's a mistake she hopes to never make again but undeniably it's been made before and there might be several garments leaving her that are on a theme. Of course, some things have been worn and loved and are now simply out of favour. What you should know, is that the things we give away will work better on someone else. It may just be the new favourite, worn-to-death thing for someone else. Give that garment a life. It's so much better than accruing dust and good intentions in our closets.

There are so many ways to give garments new homes! But if you are giving items away, think about how to do it. Organize a clothes swap with friends or community groups. Get a group together, charge a cover fee and make it a fundraiser for your school or social group! Shove it in an op shop bin, if you like, or if you support a charitable purpose, call up and find out how your closet clear out could be their selling or donating. My favourite dog charity collected clothes for a giant op shop sale event; one of my friends donates to a hospital ward that gives clothes to long-term patients that have no other options and another friend who hosts a clothes swap party with a cover charge that goes to her sporting group.

If you have the time and inclination, sell it on eBay or similar! If you are selling, make sure you clean items before listing them; the lingering smell of someone else's perfume isn't so nice. Lots of quality photos, clear measurements and a reasonable price will help you get the best return. If you are listing many things at once, make sure you tell people in the listing. Once you've sold what doesn't work for you, you can use that cash to buy things that do work.

BUILDING THE PERFECT WARDROBE

Now you've thinned out the wardrobe and you are down to what works and the things you love, make some notes. Maybe you always choose items with a clearly defined colour scheme, maybe you have all pants and no skirts or dresses (or vice versa), and maybe you always veer toward a similar fabric type, cut or style. Or, just maybe the contents of your wardrobe are a riot of all sorts! It's tempting to look at a wardrobe of all black and think you really want more colour but would you really wear it? Despite a million magazine articles on the 'must have' basics that tell us all we need to know about what to buy, we all still flounder when we're shopping for some items. And capsule wardrobes? I once spoke to a woman with only 30 items of clothing! Seriously, and that included gym clothes, work wear and casual. When I asked her how she did it, she said, "Small wardrobes don't work for everyone and are hard to pull off unless you're ok wearing stuff no one will remember (I've worn outfits two days in a row without people noticing and that's only possible because I wear no colour or patterns). You have to accept that your outfits will be boring."

Work Out What To Buy

- Find the 'holes' in your wardrobe: If you need to wear a corporate outfit every day and have two suits and three shirts, you need more work wear. If you always wear dresses but only have five, you need more dresses. If you have a whole heap of sleeveless blouses but feel cold at work, you need cardigans, blazers or sweaters. Easy right?
- If your wardrobe is mostly made up of a few colours, you can consciously stick with them, or work out which colours you could add to the colour scheme that will tone.
- If your style is thematic, such as retro/vintage, is there a point to buying things that aren't?
- If a look across your wardrobe is like a history of trends and you want to keep it that way, keep on but be mindful to toss frequently.
- If you want to develop your own style, decide which type of pieces you love now and work toward the look.

How Not To Crumple in a Heap When Buying Clothes

- Clothing store change rooms are brutal. To avoid feeling blah about your own reflection, go ahead and put on your fave makeup. Look good for you!
- Wear your ordinary knickers and bra or the ones you plan to wear with the item once you buy it. A change of underwear can really affect the fit.
- Do your hair in a style that can be messed with, no point in re doing it after each try on.
- Wear a top and bottom you love. That way if you are just trying on a top or bottom half, you get a good idea of how it will be in an outfit. Plus you are less likely to feel 'blah' when looking in mirrors.

- Bring or wear the shoes you mean to wear with the item you are buying.
- Bring a brutal but kind friend.
- Make friends with sales staff – they know their product.
- If you are not going to buy today, leave with style number, colour and size, just in case.
- Can you sit down or move your arms comfortably when you are wearing the item?
- Are you happy with the fit?

BUYING ONLINE AND FITTING AT A DISTANCE

I have no idea how I survived before online shopping! The whole world at the tap of a few buttons. Not only is it great for all your regular shopping needs, it give so much more choice. Any plus size woman will tell you that she can't get what she wants locally but local is not the end of the mall anymore. And if your passion is steam punk, pin up, rockabilly, chic geek or almost anything, it's out there! Not to mention finding those 'out of stock' jeans on ebay? Buying online can be amazing but the fit can be a painful and sometimes, costly problem. The answer is in knowing your measurements and how to use them!

A full length mirror and a tape measure is all you need. You'll need to take three main measurements. Take them while wearing your normal bra and knickers. Don't be frightened! It's just a tape measure. If you don't really want to know your measurements, and are familiar with metric then use imperial, and vice versa. Remember, this is going to help you get the right thing more often! When you wrap the tape measure around you, it should be parallel to the floor for each measurement. This is where a mirror is handy. The tape measure should be taut but not tight.

Bust: This is around the fullest part of your bust.

Waist: Everyone's waist is in a different spot but it should be above the belly button. If you are not sure, wrap some elastic around your waist and see where it settles after you've worn it for a while.

Hip: This is the fullest section of you hip area and may well include part of your butt. If you are not sure, take a few measurements. The largest one is the one you need.

What To Do With Your Measurements

Clothes have two kinds of ease, wearing ease and design ease. 'Wearing ease' is the extra amount of space you need to allow for clothes to fit; if you made clothes to fit your exact measurements they would be like a straight jacket, no room for arms to bend or to allow you to sit. 'Design ease' is the extra amount of space allowed for the style of a garment, think oversize sweaters and boyfriend jeans. I will be talking here about wearing ease. That is how much you need to add to your own measurements, when comparing them to the measurements of something you want to buy.

For Non-Stretch Fabrics: Add 7 cm/2¾ in to your measurements.

For Stretch Fabrics: For a close, second skin fit subtract 5 cm/2 in from your measurements. For a regular fit, use your exact measurements. For a more relaxed fit add 5 cm/2 in.

Use Your Most Important Measurement

If you are buying a dress made of non-stretchy fabric with a close-fitting top but a big floofy skirt, the hip measurement is not so important. The floofy skirt will allow almost any hip width but the fitted top means that the bust and waist measurement matter. You need the largest of your measurements to be accommodated. Say you have a large bust and the dress that will fit your bust will be way too big in the waist. You can either accept that it will be big in that area, get a price for tailoring or decide it just isn't for you. The same works in reverse; if you have a small bust and large waist, the bust area will be too big. For pants, the hip is most important and then the waist. Got it? It may take a little to get used to but fitting by measurement can really enhance your online shopping game.

What we wear is a glorious expression of who we are. What we wear can help us to fit in, stand out or show our membership in the club. Just remember that the garments you have, are not who you are. Wearing a certain thing will never make you a thin, Parisian model (unless you are a thin Parisian model. And you might be). Embrace who you are, show the world who you are with what you wear and never, ever have a stand-off with your wardrobe that brings you tears, makes you want to start a diet that starts with a box of chocolates and woeful regret, or gives you a sudden urge to buy impractical shoes again!

SEWING KIT

In a sea full of cheap t-shirts and fast fashion, a sewing kit may seem a little redundant. But trust me, a basic sewing kit and a few simple sewing skills can be a life saver! If you have ever been rushing off to work and noticed a missing button or a dropped hem, you'll know what I mean. If you go through your wardrobe, I'm sure there are at least a few garments you don't wear because of missing buttons, too long hems or hems that have unravelled. Knowing how to fix all that is a powerful thing. You can rescue a favourite garment, or avoid having to spend precious cash on buying a new boring work skirt or paying someone to fix the one you have. If you just can't see yourself doing it, actually sewing, I understand. I laugh when I think about all the stupid ways I've attempted to fix something, without actually sewing! I once stapled my hem when it unravelled at work. I've also tried to sticky tape my pants' hem in a similar situation. I've spent ages using iron-on hemming tape to find it unsticks and goes gross in the tumble/clothes dryer. Famously, my sister super glued a button on! Yeah, none of that is a good look at all. Sewing would have been much easier and wouldn't have looked so ghetto. So, go on, get a sewing kit...

Sew...a Needle Pulling Thread

You can find a sewing kit in many stores and they can be pretty good quality, but often they contain poor quality items that will frustrate you more than they should. Head to your local sewing and craft store, or to a variety or department store that has a selection of sewing and haberdashery items. This simple kit will get you through the repairs I'm going to cover:

Safety pins, a good handful in various sizes.
Sewing thread – black, white, very pale grey or taupe, red and any other colour/s you wear often.
Hand sewing needles – you can usually get packs with various sizes.
Small sharp scissors.
Quick unpick/seam ripper.
Sewing pins.
Tape measure.
Some sort of cute makeup bag or pencil case to store it all in.
Optional but helpful when taking up hems:
  Tailors/sewing chalk.
  Water erasable fabric marker.
  Fabric scissors.

Emergency Mending Tip

Carrying a few safety pins in your handbag is super handy for on-the-go, get-through-the-day repairs. You can use them to hold up a hem, fix a gaping shirt, hold up a zipper that just won't stay, keep bra straps from peeking out and manage total wardrobe malfunctions. And you may well make new friends in the ladies' room when you can provide a safety pin for a broken dress strap!

Fixing a Hem

Before you get started, press the hem so it's sitting nicely (see Pressing).

Put the end of the thread in one hand and the spool in the other and stretch out your arms. Measure and cut a length of thread as long as your arm span. Thread the needle and knot the two cut ends together. This is the longest you want your thread to be when you are sewing with your thread doubled. If it's much longer, you will find it tangles and makes life hard.

It's best to start sewing at a seam (inner leg on pants) to conceal your threads. Start by hiding your thread knot on the inside of the garment, and bring your needle up through the underside of the fold. If your knot pulls through, just make a couple of knots, on top of the first and try again.

Move the needle over diagonally and catch just a few threads of the fabric above the fold with your needle. The less fabric you pick up, the more invisible it will be from the right side. If you can, try to pick up only one thread. I know it doesn't seem like it will hold safely but you'd be surprised.

Then swivel the needle and come back up through the fold.

Continue just picking up single threads and coming back up through the fold diagonally.

Keep your stitches evenly spaced and lined up. It can be hard to eyeball an even distance so I use my index finger or thumbnail as guide. Remember to keep your pick-up stitches small, just a thread or two.

When you run out of thread or you are finished, pick up a few fold threads with your needle and pull the thread through, but not all the way. Slide your needle through the loop you have created and pull tight. Repeat and trim your threads.

Voila! Admire your neat work and feel proud that you hemmed it yourself!

Fix a Half Undone Hem: Have a good look at the stitching that remains, give it a gentle tug. If it seems secure enough, start sewing over the good stitiching, working your way over the missing stitching. You should overlap the good stitching by at least 3 cm/1¼ in on each side. Most of the time you are better off doing the whole thing.

Thread Tips

- It's unlikely that you are going to have a rainbow of sewing threads that perfectly match every sewing scenario. Take out the colour you think is closest, unspool a bit of thread so you have a single strand and lay it on the garment and see how it will look. Sometimes the colour can be deceiving when it's on the spool. If you are going to buy thread, be sure to take the garment with you to the store! In a pinch, a very light grey or taupe will blend in much better than you think.
- If you buy thread in a sewing store, there will be a scary number of choices! Not only in colour but different threads for different situations. Anything marked for hand sewing is a good choice, be it cotton, polycotton or silk. 'All sew' thread (designed for sewing machines) is perfectly fine too but tends to kink more than hand-sewing thread.

Take Up a Hem

There are a few ways to take up a hem. I'm going to give you a couple of straightforward options, for when something just needs shortening by the depth of the hem (folding) and when it needs reducing a lot (cutting). First, you need to work out where you want your hem to be. It can be really helpful to have a friend mark the fabric, but I'm going to give you some tips for going solo.

Grab your garment and try it on with the shoes you plan to wear with it. Have a look in the mirror and get an idea of where things should be. If you have a friend conveniently close, get them to mark the spot with a pin. If not, take off the garment and estimate the spot, then pin it up with a safety pin (too much on and off for sewing pins, you'll just prick yourself). Try your garment on again and check it in the mirror. Repeat until perfection is achieved!

Now you have your mark, you'll know if you need to fold up the hem once or if more drastic action is required. If you are folding, just follow the Fixing A Hem instructions. If more drastic action is needed, grab your chalk/marker, tape measure, sewing pins and fabric scissors.

Turn the garment inside out, being sure not to lose the 'pin marker' for your desired length. If your pin is holding several layers, carefully reposition it so when you are looking at your inside-out garment you can see it but everything is hanging as normal.

Look at the hem of your garment, measure its depth. Let's say it's 2.5 cm/1 in deep. From your pin, measure down (toward the existing hem) a distance that is double the hem depth (in my example, that's 5 cm/2 in). Mark this new measurement on the garment with your chalk/ marker – that's where you will eventually cut. This is called the hem allowance. If you just cut where your original mark is you won't have any space to make a new hem. The hem allowance gives you the space from the cut raw edge to fold up the depth of the hem (2.5 cm/1 in) once, and then again.

If you don't have enough space to keep the original hem depth, you can either unpick the hem to create some or choose a smaller hem depth. Anything smaller than 1 cm/½ in will be nearly impossible with this simple method.

Measure the distance from your 'cut mark' to the bottom of the existing hem. Mark this distance, measuring from the bottom of the existing hem, all the way around the hem (both legs, if pants/trousers). You should now have a dashed cutting line, you can fill it in or use it as is.

Take a deep breath and cut on the cutting line.

Use an iron to press the hem up the amount you measured earlier; 2.5 cm/1 in in our example. You want this to be accurate, so measure as you go and press cleanly. Once you have pressed up the hem all the way around, repeat the process again to make a double hem. The cut edge should be neatly folded away.

Follow the sewing directions for Fixing a Hem.

Sewing On a Button

There are two kinds of buttons, flat buttons with holes in them and shank buttons with a loop at the back. Both are really simple to sew on. If you are sewing on a flat button with four holes, check which way the rest of the buttons are sewn on. It will either be an X shape or an = shape, make sure you sew yours on to match.

Flat Buttons

Measure and cut a length of thread about as long as the distance from your hand to your shoulder. Thread the needle and knot the two cut ends together. This is enough thread to sew a button or two.

Poke your needle from the back of the fabric, through to the front, where you want the button to be. Thread your needle through one of the buttonholes, so the button is resting on the fabric.

Put your needle through one of the other buttonholes (keep in mind if you are making an X or a =) and down though the fabric to the back.

Come back up through the fabric at the first buttonhole and then down through the second hole and the fabric again. If you are sewing a button with only two holes, you should do this a total of eight times. If you are sewing a four-hole button, do this four times for the first set of holes and then four times for the second set of holes.

Bring the needle up through the fabric but not through the button. Your needle and thread should be between the fabric and the button.

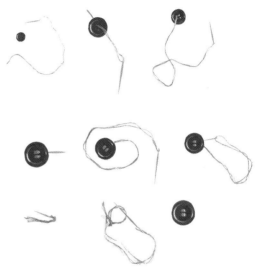

Wrap the thread around the button, three times and push the needle to the back of the fabric. This creates a shank, a little spacer to help the button sit up off the fabric and makes it much easier to fit through buttonholes.

Now that you are on the back, take a tiny little stitch of fabric and pull the thread through, but not all the way. Slide your needle through the loop you have created and pull tight. Repeat and trim your threads.

Admire your button, back in its rightful place!

Shank Buttons

Measure and cut a length of thread, about as long as the distance from your hand to your shoulder. Thread the needle and knot the two cut ends together. This is enough thread to sew on a button or two.

Poke your needle from the back of the fabric, through to the front, where you want the button to be. Thread your needle through the shank loop, so the button is resting on the fabric.

Push your needle back down through the fabric, close to where you came up.

Come back up through the fabric, through the shank loop and back down through the fabric. Repeat another seven times.

Now that you are on the back, take a tiny little stitch of fabric and pull the thread through, but not all the way. Slide your needle through the loop you have created and pull tight. Repeat and trim your threads.

Admire your button, back in its rightful place!

Button Tip

You know those spare buttons that sometimes come with clothes in a little plastic bag, on the swing tag? Save those. Put them in your sewing kit. Obviously they are handy when fixing the garment they came from but sometimes they are handy for fixing something else too. Trust me when I say that matching a button is a pain, much harder than you imagine, so it really is handy. But if you can't match a button, consider changing every other one or all of them for some new ones. It's a great save for a beloved shirt but it can also really personalize a garment or make it over entirely.

PRESS TO IMPRESS

There are times and places where you really have to get the iron out and press something to crisp perfection such as for job interviews, or jobs that have a corporate uniform, or jobs that require corporate dress. And then there's cheating… Both are valid options in the right circumstance. I'll go through both. You can test your results and find what works for you. Please don't skip ironing in work situations, it's super important to present professionally. Whichever you use, please be sure to check the laundry symbol tag on the garment and choose appropriate processes/heat settings.

Cheating

- If you remove garments from the dryer when they are dry but before the cool down setting, sometimes you can avoid pressing.
- Spritz a wrinkled garment with water and throw it in a hot dryer (on its own) for 10–20 minutes while you do your hair and makeup. Great for busy mornings.
- Hang a garment in the bathroom while you take a shower and let the steam relax the wrinkles. This works well on delicate, no-iron garments and flimsy fabrics. Handy in a pinch or while travelling.
- Give wet clothes a good shake out and hang on hangers, before hanging on the line.
- Button up any buttons and zip zippers.
- Steam with a clothes steamer, you can find cheap hand-held ones on eBay and Amazon.

IRONING

Before you get started, you'll need a few things – iron, ironing board, spray bottle filled with water, hangers and a place to hang things.

Fill the water reservoir with water (see Iron Cleaning) and set your iron to the correct temperature setting. Wait until the iron heats to the right temperature, usually there is an indicator light that will let you know. Irons can be super-hot in the heat up process; if you don't wait you can risk scorching.

Place your garment over the ironing board and move the iron over it. Always keep the iron moving; never let it sit still over any part of the garment. If there's a stubborn wrinkle that refuses to iron out, use the steam button to steam it out and/or spray some water on it and iron. Begin with the larger areas and finish with the corners. Once you iron a section, move the garment away from you. If you move it towards you, it may wrinkle as you lean over it and possibly push it against the ironing board.

The ironing board is shaped to help you get around the different shapes in garments but not sleeves. You can buy special sleeve boards (often used by those who sew) but a rolled up hand towel works too. Just roll it up, place it inside the sleeve and iron.

Hang each garment carefully after you press it, you don't want to wrinkle it again. Once you are all done be sure to turn off the iron and tip out any leftover water.

Tips For Pressing Like a Pro

Press Cloths: A press cloth is a wonderful thing. It's essentially just a piece of fabric you put between the item you are about to press and the iron. Ever pressed something and made it go all shiny? Or left the shape of an iron on a delicate fabric? Or had gunk come out of the iron and leave a mark? Or worst of all, melted the fabric? A press cloth helps to protect against all of that. A new but washed 100 percent cotton or linen tea towel will certainly do the trick but don't use a tea towel from the kitchen! I can tell you from experience that even very old, very small chocolate stains can ruin a garment. Old sheets and pillowcases can work well too. Try to pick fabrics that don't have too much texture, you don't want to press the pattern of the weave into your garment. The bonus of this kind of cloth is that it can be dampened before use to create extra steam.

Velvet, Cord and Textured Fabrics: If possible, avoid pressing these fabrics and steam them instead. If you must press them, place them textured side down on a fluffy towel and press lightly to avoid crushing them.

Small Space Ironing: If space is tight, it is worth investing in a small bench top ironing board. At a pinch, a towel folded in half and arranged on a kitchen bench will work as an ironing surface.

Ironing Pleats: Use paper clips (plain metal ones, NOT coated ones) to secure the pleat in place at the hem before ironing. Simply remove when done.

Styling Safe and Cosmetic Cleans

I'll bet you have some heated hairstyling tools – a straightener, hot rollers, curling iron? Ever cleaned them? I don't know about you but I don't love hair breakage or using gunky tools. I also don't like breakouts and clogged makeup brushes either. Cleaning and sanitizing these items is so easy, you'll be wondering why you never did it before.

HOW TO CLEAN HEATED HAIR APPLIANCES

Heated hair styling tools are great at giving your hair volume or smoothing it out but it is wickedly easy to scorch bathroom counters and carpets, for example) or actually set the house on fire, by leaving them on flammable surfaces! So here are a few safety tips;

- Rest heated hair tools on a flat silicon pot holder (designed to take the heat) to reduce the risk of scorching the surface below.
- Consider adding a timer to the plug where you use your heated styling tools, that way they will turn off automatically.
- Consider getting a heat-resistant travel pouch to put your tools in before leaving the house. Or invest in one of those spiral metal stands to rest them in.

Cleaning heat styling tools regularly is a good habit to have for a few reasons. Build up from styling products and heat protectants can snag your hair, leading to frizz and even breakage (oh no!). Removing the build up is beneficial for your hair and can extend the life of the tool itself. If you already have quite a build up, you may need to repeat the method below until the build up is removed. If you use a heat-styling tool every day, clean it every 7-14 days. This process will also sanitize your tools, so clean them before and after letting someone use your appliances. A friend chucked her GHD hair straightener because of gunk that could have been removed. Don't let it happen to you!

Cleaning Straighteners/Flat Irons, Curling Wands/Irons and Crimpers: Make sure that the styling tool is cool, switched off and unplugged. Moisten a soft cloth (a piece of old towel or face cloth would be perfect) in isopropyl alcohol. You don't want so much alcohol that it drips or seeps inside the device. Gently rub the plates/barrel until any visible gunk has been removed. Allow to dry completely before use.

Cleaning Hot Rollers: Make sure that the rollers are cool, off and unplugged.

Use canned air (the kind that you find in office supply stores for cleaning keyboards) to remove any dust or hair from the base. Moisten a soft cloth (a piece of old towel or face cloth would be perfect) in isopropyl alcohol. You don't want so much alcohol that it drips or seeps inside the device. Gently wipe over the base unit. If the rollers are plastic, use the alcohol-moistened cloth or a clean, soft toothbrush dipped in alcohol to remove any hair or hair product. Be careful to avoid dampening the connection pins on the roller. If the rollers are covered in velvety fabric, rub them with a clean, soft, dry toothbrush to loosen any product. If you wish to sanitize them, spray them with isopropyl alcohol, avoiding the connection pins. Allow to dry completely before putting the rollers back on the base and before use.

HAPPY HAIRBRUSHES

When you brush your hair, your brush gets coated in scalp oils, skin, hair and product. Brushes can also get pretty dusty. You put all that effort into keeping your locks clean and shiny, it makes sense to keep your brushes clean.

You'll need a few things:
Tail/sectioning comb
Scissors
Towel
Old toothbrush (optional)
Baby or clarifying shampoo or dish-washing liquid

Start by removing as much hair and dust as you can. Use the tail of the comb to weave between the bristles to lift up the hair. Use scissors to cut the hair, so that it can be peeled away from the brush.

Once most of the hair is out, use the teeth of the comb to brush out any remaining hair, lint and dust. Just a warning here – you may bend the tines of your comb, so please don't use an irreplaceable favourite!

Now it's time to give your brush a wash in warm, soapy water. Different brushes need slightly different approaches.

Brushes With a Solid Plastic Core and Plastic or Nylon Bristles can be soaked and scrubbed as much as you like in warm soapy water. Use the toothbrush to scrub between the bristles too. Rinse well.

Solid Metal or Plastic Combs can be soaked and scrubbed as much as you like in warm soapy water. Use the toothbrush to scrub between the bristles too. Rinse well.

Brushes That Have a Domed, Air-Filled, Rubbery Pad that will fill with water if soaked. Dip the bristles in shallow soapy water, scrub carefully, re soap and rinse.

Wooden-Handled or Boar Bristle Brushes: Do your best to keep the handle dry. Dip the bristles in shallow soapy water, scrub carefully, re soap and rinse.

Lay your brushes, bristle side down, on a clean towel to dry. If you want to sanitize your brushes once they are dry, spritz with alcohol and allow to dry before use.

MAKEUP BRUSH MAKEOVER

Sometimes we forget to clean and sanitize the things we use every day. Cleaning your makeup brushes regularly is important and really only takes minutes. Remember that every time you use a brush you put oil, product and bacteria on it – not to mention dust if the product is kept in the open. Dirty brushes can make your make up look muddy, spread bacteria, causing breakout, and shorten the life of products.

Daily Cleaning

Keep a spray bottle of makeup brush cleaner (lots of brands have inexpensive versions) or even a spray bottle of rubbing or isopropyl alcohol handy.

After you use a brush, spray it and rub it gently back and forth on a paper towel. Paper towel won't leave as much lint as tissue and the texture helps remove product. You can also use an old bath towel or a face cloth but be sure to wash it often.

Repeat until no colour comes off on the towel.

DEEP CLEANING

This should be done every week or two, depending on how often you use your brushes. Also, see the list of situations to sanitize in the makeup Sanitize It section. Don't forget the brushes and sponges lurking in makeup bags or inside compacts! Be careful not to wet too much the metal clasp (the ferrule) that holds the bristles in place. Water that is trapped under there can weaken the glue holding the bristles and cause them to fall out. You can buy a variety of cake and liquid brush cleansers but foaming facial cleansers, baby shampoo or dish-washing liquid will do the trick.

Put a drop or two of cleanser in the palm of your hand or on a textured, silicon oven mitt.

Wet the brush with lukewarm water and swirl the bristles in the cleanser in your palm or mitt.

Rinse under running water until the water runs clear. Be sure to remove all the cleanser, feel the bristles to check.

Place on a clean towel or on paper towel to dry overnight. It's important not to store them wet or stand them upright while wet as that can cause water to get under the ferrule.

Sponges and Beauty Blenders

The cheap sponges from pharmacies and supermarkets don't really have much of a shelf life and will start to fall apart after a few washes. They make great disposables and are handy on the go but don't expect them to last. Beauty blenders tend to be sturdier and can survive for ages, but be careful not to damage them with your nails! Bacteria just loves sponges, so wash them after each use and make sure to wash the ones in compacts in your bag too.

Dip your sponge in water and then rub in some cleanser. Get a good lather and be sure to work the product out of the sponge. When finished, rinse the sponge thoroughly with water and allow it to air dry.

See, that was super easy! And now you have nice, clean brushes and sponges ready for action.

FIX IT, SANITIZE IT OR TOSS IT!

Toss It

Old makeup can be crawling with bacteria. It really isn't worth the risk. Do you know how long you should keep your makeup? Many products have a little symbol with a number that indicates the number of months it can be used safely after opening. But if you're not sure…

Mascara: Toss your mascara after 3 months.

Eye Pencils: Eye pencils can be kept up to 2 years. Be sure to sharpen before each application.

Eye Shadows: Cream shadows should last 12 months. Powder shadows will keep 2 years or more.

Lipsticks: You can keep your lippies and your lip pencils for 2 years. As with eye pencils, sharpen your lip pencils before each use.

Blushers and Powders: Chuck your cream blushers after a year, powder blushes and powders after 2 years.

Foundations and Concealers: Moisturizing foundations and stick concealers can hang around for 18 months. A 12-month shelf life applies to both oil-free foundations, which can dry out quickly and liquid concealers.

Sunscreen: These have expiry dates; chuck when expired.

If your makeup separates, dries out, or starts to look or smell funny, it's definitely time to replace it. Using clean brushes and sponges will help lengthen the life of your cosmetics. Be sure to wash or replace your applicators frequently.

Sanitize It!

Keeping your makeup clean makes sense, no one wants to rub bacteria on their face. So, when should you sanitize yours?

- Before you use the product on anyone else.
- After anyone else uses the product.
- When selling, swapping or giving away.
- After illness or infections.
- After a breakout.
- If a bumpy or shiny texture develops in a powder product (that's oil from your face, transferred to the product).

Avoid Cross-Contamination by Using a Spatula Instead of Your Finger: If you have a pot of moisturizer, foundation or any makeup product you use by digging it out with your fingers, you may want to get a small makeup spatula. They are inexpensive and readily available. Just take the product you need out with the spatula and place it either on your hand or a small palette and work from there, refilling with a scoop from the clean spatula as necessary. It's quite simple and keeps your products clean.

Sanitize Pressed Shadows and Other Pressed Powders: Gently rub away the top most layer of product with a tissue. Spray with rubbing alcohol and allow to dry with the compact open.

Cleaning Your Lipstick: Carefully wind your lipstick tube up and wipe off the top layer of lipstick with a tissue. Then spray with alcohol and allow to dry before winding the lipstick down. You can also spray the packaging.

Cream Concealers or Shadows in Pots or Palettes: Gently rub away the top most layer of product with a tissue. Spray with rubbing alcohol and allow to dry with the compact open.

Lip and Eye Pencils: The best way to keep pencils clean is to sharpen them before each use but they can also be sprayed with alcohol after sharpening. For retractable pencils, wind them up a touch and spray with alcohol.

Fix It

These fixes work often (not always) but if there is a chance to save a precious product, I say take it! Some of these fixes rely on you having a container to use, you can buy inexpensive lip gloss pots, eye shadow pans and palettes but you can also use old ones you have around. If you are reusing a container, clean it thoroughly, allow to dry, spritz with rubbing or isopropyl alcohol and dry again.

Melted Lipsticks: Trust me when I say hot cars and your favourite lippie are not friends! If you've melted your lipstick you can either use a clean knife to scrape it into a jar or melt it into a jar. To melt, scrape the lipstick into a large spoon and hold over the flame of a candle until only just melted and pour into the jar. Just apply with a lip brush.

Broken Pressed Shadows Powders: For cracks and breaks that leave the pan almost whole, spray generously with rubbing or isopropyl alcohol and use a clean tool to press it back to shape. If you are in shatter city, grind the powder to a fine dust with no chunks, using a clean spoon and small bowl. Then follow the steps for converting a loose powder to pressed, below.

Convert a Loose Shadow or Powder to a Pressed One: Add the powder to a small, clean bowl and have a clean spoon handy. Add rubbing or isopropyl alcohol (the kind we are using for cleaning), a drop at a time, until a thick but smooth paste forms. Spoon the paste into the container and press it in. A final press with a paper towel adds a decorative texture to the final powder. Allow to dry, compact open for 24 hours minimum, it needs to be 100 percent dry.

Championing the Household Chores

Appliance Maintenance

OMG!!! I've only had it for a year but now it's…

I hate to break this to you but you have to maintain your appliances. They need cleaning and looking after, just now and again, so they can provide you with clean clothes or golden brown toast or clean dishes. Maintenance seems boring but a little attention now may prevent having to buy a new appliance sooner than you'd rather. Because let's face it, it's more fun to spend your money on shoes rather than having to replace a toaster or pay the washing machine repair man. As we all know and can attest, having to replace an item always comes at exactly the worst moment!

HOW TO CLEAN YOUR IRON

Goopy bits on the sole plate? Are you ironing crud onto your clothes?
Start with a cold, unplugged iron. Use a sponge, dipped in warm, soapy (dish-washing liquid) water to rub at the soleplate.

If that hasn't got the goop off, dip a clean cloth in white vinegar and give the soleplate a good rub. Rinse the iron off with a clean cloth dipped in water.
For super-stubborn crud, sprinkle 1-2 tablespoons of regular salt on a paper towel, on top of your ironing board. Heat your iron to the cotton setting and gently press/iron the salt until the iron is clean.

Cruddy white bits coming out of your iron or floating in your steam water?
Fill the reservoir of your cold iron at least one quarter of the way with white vinegar. Turn the iron on and place it on the steam setting. Steam the iron onto clean rag until the reservoir is completely empty. Fill the reservoir with clean water and steam the rag again. Rinse the reservoir thoroughly with clean water by filling it completely and then emptying it completely.

Using demineralised water (or water that has been boiled and cooled) will keep the reservoir much cleaner than if you use tap water. Just run through the cleaning process as often as needed. Don't forget to empty your water out before storing the iron!

HOW TO CLEAN YOUR WASHING MACHINE

I know, I know, I know! A washing machine cleans things, how come I need to clean it too?
Basically they get icky – soap, fabric softener, minerals, lint and sometimes mildew can build

up. And if you don't get to it you can end up with smelly clothes, instead of fresh, clean laundry. Plus, think of all the filth that gets swilled around in there, ick! It's pretty easy to do and I have instructions for top and front loaders.

1. Add 250 ml (8 fl oz/ 1 cup) of bleach and nothing else to the machine on the HOTTEST temperature and run it through its fullest, longest cycle. If you have a top loader you can let the cycle start to mix the bleach through the water and then stop it and allow to soak for 30 minutes before running the rest of the cycle. Most front loaders have a tub clean cycle you can use for this. It could be happening while you are flipping pancakes on a Saturday.

2. Clean out any lint filters and under the seals on front loaders.

3. Remove any parts that are removable and wash in warm soapy water. Some top loaders have removable fabric softener or bleach trays and front loaders will have a removable soap/softener/bleach tray.

4. Put everything back together. Add 250 ml (8 fl oz/ 1 cup) of white vinegar and 115 g (4 oz/½ cup) of bicarbonate of soda to the machine. Once again run through the fullest, longest, HOTTEST cycle. This is an excellent time to paint your nails or read a magazine.

5. Mix up a solution of 1 part white vinegar and 1 part water and use a clean cloth to clean the exterior of the machine and anywhere that would not have gotten cleaned by the standard cycle.

6. Stand back and admire your fresh smelling, germ-free machine. And remember to do this every 3 months to keep it that way.

HOW TO CLEAN YOUR CLOTHES/TUMBLE DRYER

Dryers are one of those appliances that vary around the world. The most common kind simply plugs in and does not have an outside vent. The section below applies to all dryers but the kind with an outside vent has some extra steps that I'll add at the end. Whichever type you own, you should think about cleaning your dryer every 3-6 months, depending on use. Not doing this literally starts fires. It's not exciting but just do it, okay?

Dryers have a lint trap that should be cleared after each use. Start by pulling this out, removing any lint and giving the removed parts a good wash. Use warm soapy water with a little bit of vinegar (about 125 ml (4 fl oz/½ cup) per kitchen sink full of water) to help remove any film from fabric softener etc. Dry completely before replacing.

Clean any build up around the lint trap. Depending on the dryer, a damp cloth may be all you need, or you may need to grab the vacuum. You can angle the vacuum's crevice tool (that pointy sort of attachment) into where the lint trap sits but don't force!

Dampen a cloth with a 50/50 water and vinegar mix and wipe over the inner bowl, door and under/around the rubber door seals. Wipe over the exterior.

For dryers that have a plumbed vent: Detach the dryer lint duct and clean it out, or vacuum it out. Check the outside vent by lifting the flap and make sure there isn't any debris or lint blocking the vent, preventing air from escaping freely.

HOW TO CLEAN YOUR KETTLE

Gross floaty bits in your tea or coffee? Minerals can build up in your kettle and this can result in a taste or even little mineral flakes in your drink! This is any easy way to descale your kettle, you should give this a go every month if you use your kettle a lot or have hard water, and every 2-3 months if you don't.

I clean my kettle with lemon, cut it up into wedges and drop into the kettle, boil it and discard the water, then re-boil with just water and discard it.
OR
White vinegar is great, 125 ml (4 fl oz/½ cup) in a full kettle of water, boil it, discard and then re-boil with just water and discard it.

HOW TO CLEAN YOUR TOASTER

If your toaster smells burn-y for no reason or it's just starting to look grungy, it's time to clean the toaster. Cleaning the toaster can create a few crumbs, so work over the sink or put some newspaper on the bench/worktop. Also, if you are cleaning your floors, do it after you have done the toaster! Start with a completely cold toaster that is switched off and unplugged.

Most toasters have a crumb tray in the bottom, it should just slide out. Don't worry if yours doesn't, we will get the crumbs out anyway. Shake off the crumbs and give the tray a good wash in soapy water and allow to dry. Turn the toaster upside down and gently shake out all the crumbs. This can take a few goes! Use a pastry brush to remove any crumbs around the toast slots. Moisten a cloth with warm soapy water and clean the outside. If you have any stubborn gunk, add a little white vinegar to your cloth.

HOW TO CLEAN YOUR DISHWASHER

Think of all that food that swishes around in your dishwasher. Think of the bits that get stuck in the dishwasher and rot. Not pretty, huh? That's why cleaning your dishwasher is a no brainer. If your dishwasher hasn't been doing a good job lately, maybe it just needs a clean. This cleaning plan will remove any hunks of food, mould or mildew and help to clean the pipes and other bits you can't see.

Start by removing the dish racks and cutlery sorter. Remove any food or obstacles (lost drink bottle lids for example) from the bottom of the dishwasher. Grab a bowl of hot, soapy water and a cloth. You might want an old toothbrush too. Clean the detergent compartment and all around the door. Basically, you need to clean all the areas where the water doesn't swish around freely or any areas that have visible filth. Once you are done, replace the racks and cutlery sorter. Fill the detergent compartment with bicarbonate of soda (baking soda), pour 500 ml (17 fl oz/2 cups) of white vinegar into the bottom of the dishwasher and run the dishwasher on it's hottest cycle. Do this every 3 months to keep your dishwasher sparkling.

HOW TO CLEAN YOUR REFRIGERATOR

This one of those jobs that just has to be done from time to time but it's a great way to clean a second-hand refrigerator before putting your edibles into it!

Cleaning the refrigerator is best done before you go shopping. That way you can throw out anything that has expired and also because you will have less to move. Remove the food from one shelf. Remove the shelf or rack and wash it in warm soapy water and dry well. It can be easier to do in a laundry sink or bath if you have one. Before you put it back, wipe over the 'walls' of the refrigerator with a cloth dampened in warm soapy water and a dash of vinegar. Keep working in sections until the inside is clean. For more refrigerator tips, see the section on Food Storage.

HOW TO CLEAN YOUR OVEN

I fully admit I don't clean my oven as often as I should but you better believe that a landlord will want to see a clean oven when they inspect the property. If you are cleaning your oven for an inspection, I recommend doing it a couple of days before hand so that you can ensure any bicarbonate of soda residue is cleaned off. I know that caustic, one wipe oven cleaners seem tempting but I know people who have had terrible reactions to them and others who found they just didn't work well. Plus, I once moved into a house where there was so much residue on the oven that it burned off toxic fumes for two months, no matter how many time I rinsed it over!

Make sure the oven is cold and off and if your oven has a storage compartment, remove everything from it. Get the racks soaking first. Remove the oven racks and put them in the bath or laundry tub (anything big enough to contain the racks) with enough hot water to cover. Add a good squeeze of dish-washing liquid (about 1 tablespoon), 1 cup (225 g/8 oz) of bicarbonate of soda (baking soda) and 250 ml (8 fl oz/1 cup) of white vinegar. Let them soak while you clean the oven.

To clean the oven interior, spray the ceiling, sides, door and floor of the oven liberally with white vinegar and dust generously with bicarbonate of soda. Allow to sit for 30 minutes. Get a bucket of soapy water and a scrubbing brush. Dip the brush in the water and start scrubbing the floor of the oven. You can spritz with white vinegar as needed. Once you have the floor clean, use a dustpan and brush to remove the excess bicarb. Don't be too perfect, because you are going to make more mess doing the sides and ceiling. Continue on to the rest of the oven, rinsing your brush often. Once you've got the whole oven done, wipe over with a damp cloth, rinsing and repeating until all of the bicarb residue is gone.

May this instructional section save you repairs and replacements. If you have invested your hard-earned cash into a quality appliance (or been gifted one), it's very much worth looking after. If you've ever suffered sudden appliance death, you'll know it always comes at the worst moments. A favourite top shredded in the wash, an interview outfit in need of drying in the depths of winter and a dead dryer, a dead kettle on the earliest of mornings. Once you have moved into your first home, it becomes an extension of you. Care for your things with the same attention you care for yourself. Not only will you keep in the good graces of landlords and avoid your mates thinking you're a pig, there is a great satisfaction in knowing everything is clean and lovely. That is, clean and lovely for you to enjoy!

Spring Cleaning and Landlord Inspections

I am a reformed cleaning product junkie. If a product promised me shiny surfaces, or promised to banish soap scum with a single spray, I bought it. I loved a miracle in a bottle. But then I was disappointed in the results. There was always some muscle power required and the contents of the bottles smelled terrible and sometimes I got dizzy. My Mum was the queen of chemical clean until a doctor told her that these products were the cause of her crippling headaches. I had no faith in 'green cleaning' (that is cleaning without harsh chemicals, the way our great grandmothers did) until I tried it. So, I will understand if you are sceptical. But the products that I now use work better than any miracle promise in a can ever did. When I talk cleaning and sanitizing, the items listed below are the things I use. If you want to go your own way and use other cleaning products, feel free. But I dare you to compare results and see. These products aren't just for regular cleaning either – they'll help you restore a burned saucepan, clean up spilled almost anything on the carpet and even fix a smashed eye shadow!

Rubbing Alcohol/Isopropyl Alcohol: Found in chemists/pharmacies/drug stores. The 90 per cent alcohol version is the best; higher percentages will evaporate too quickly to fully sanitize or to achieve full sanitization. Keep some in a clearly labelled plastic spray bottle. Clear, alcohol-based hand sanitizer can sometimes be substituted at a pinch and I mention where that is appropriate. In most countries, this is sold over the counter, if you have trouble finding it, ask your pharmacist.

Bicarb/Bicarbonate of Soda/Baking Soda: Found in the baking isle of the supermarket/grocery store. Keep some in a shaker type container with big holes in the lid, but that also seals to be airtight – a repurposed plastic Parmesan cheese shaker is ideal.

Lemons/Lemon Juice: Always use fresh lemons for cleaning purposes. The bottled kind can contain ingredients that may stain. If you don't have lemon, then white vinegar is your pal.

White Vinegar: Found in the supermarket/grocery store. Plain old white vinegar is the kind you want. I always have a 2 litres (3½ pints) bottle on hand. Keep some in a clearly labelled plastic spray bottle. The absolute cheapest kind is just fine.

The rule of cleaning, whether you are using more natural cleaners or straight up chemicals is – **always test in an inconspicuous spot!** You never know how the surface to be cleaned will react to the product, therefore always test a cleaning method in a small, less visible spot before proceeding.

PRODUCT JUNKIE

Washing Powder or Liquid: It really depends on your washing machine. Is it top loading, front loading, energy or water saving? Front loaders require a low suds detergent, the package should say that it is safe for front loaders. You can put either type of detergent in a top loader, in fact many formulations can be used in both top and front loaders. If you use cold water to wash or have a water or energy saving machine, liquid is a good choice because it dissolves better. As long as you're buying the right type for your machine, choose whatever you like.

Soakers/Enzyme Cleaners/Colour Safe Whiteners: These are not a 'must have' but can be really helpful at removing stains and smells. I like the enzyme-based kind because they can be a handy cleaning tool and not just in your laundry.

Bleach: Also not a must have but handy if you have white sheets, towels or a white shower curtain.

Fabric Softener: Fabric softeners can smell wonderful but they can coat fabrics and irritate the skin. They will make towels and sheets less absorbent too. I substitute them with white vinegar, which keeps fabric soft and helps to shift grease too. Just put 1 cupfull in the wash. You can use softener if you like it but try and resist using it on your towels.

DEEP CLEAN

I've never met anyone who really enjoys cleaning (or maybe you are that person). My aim here is to make things as quick, easy and painless as possible. I also mention how to clean areas that landlords like to see sparkling and troubleshoot some of those tricky problems such as carpet stains, mould and mildew. If you really hate to clean but want a shiny house, the secret is to do a little every day. Trust me, you'll be astonished by what 15 minutes of putting things away and 15 minutes of actual cleaning per day can achieve. If you have a landlord inspection, are moving out or in, are having house guests or are in need of a spring clean, follow these cleaning methods to the Spring Clean Checklist. From the Saturday morning roundup to a full blown clean, follow these steps to a glorious, clean home!

LAUNDRY SYMBOLS GUIDE

⊟ ⊟	1 dot = cool, 2 dots = warm, 3 dots = hot or iron at degree setting
⊔	Machine wash at this temperature
△	Bleach can be used
⊠	Do not wash
Ⓐ	Dry clean
○	Dry clean with care
Ⓕ	Dry clean in white spirit or solvent 113, needs special care
⊓	Hang to dry
👆	Hand wash only
▲✕	Do not bleach
⊠	Do not iron
⊠	Do not tumble dry
⊡	Improved with tumble drying
⊗	Do not dry clean
Ⓟ	Dry clean in perchlo-rethylene white spirit, solvent 113 or 11
⫾⫾⫾	Drip dry

A TO Z OF LAUNDRY STAINS

Blood: Make a paste of salt and lemon juice (or water and enzyme soaker and apply by dabbing on the marks and then wash as normal in COLD water.

Chocolate: Apply undiluted dish-washing liquid to marks and wait 1O minutes and then wash as normal in COLD water.

Coffee: Apply undiluted dish-washing liquid and wait for 30 minutes and wash as normal.

Deodorant: Make a paste of enzyme soaker and water. Apply to the marks, and then wait 30 minutes and wash as normal.

Fruit: Apply undiluted dish-washing liquid. Wait for 30 minutes and wash as normal. Dry in the sun where possible.

Grass: Make a paste of salt and lemon juice (or water and enzyme soaker) and dab on the marks. Wait 30 minutes and wash as normal.

Grease: Apply undiluted dish-washing liquid to marks and wait 10 minutes and then wash as normal.

Makeup: Apply undiluted dish-washing liquid to marks and, then wait 30 minutes and wash as normal.

Mud: Apply undiluted dish-washing liquid to marks and wait 10 minutes and then wash as normal.

Nail Polish: Dab with acetone on a clean cloth (not nail polish remover). Apply undiluted dish-washing liquid and wash as normal.

Paint: Apply methylated spirit to both sides and apply by rubbing into of mark and wash as normal.

Pen/Ink: Spray with hairspray or white vinegar or dab marks with glycerine and wash as normal.

Red Wine: Make a paste of bicarb and white vinegar wait 30 minutes and wash as normal.

Rust: Make a paste of salt and lemon juice (or water and enzyme soaker) and apply by dabbing on marks and wait 30 minutes and wash as normal.

Sweat: Soak in 1 litre (1¾ pints) water and 500 ml (17 fl oz/ 2 cups) vinegar, then wait 30 minutes and wash as normal with 225 g (8 oz/ 1 cup) bicarb and 250 ml (8 fl oz/ 1 cup) white vinegar added at the beginning of the wash. Dry in the sun where possible.

Urine: Apply undiluted dish-washing liquid to marks and wait 30 minutes and wash as normal with 1 cup (250 ml/8 fl oz) white vinegar added at beginning of wash.

THINGS UP HIGH

Fabric Lampshades: Most dust can be removed with a lint roller. If it is an easily removable shade you can vacuum it with the upholstery attachment or blast with a hairdryer on cool. Wipe any marks with a damp cloth and voila!

Glass Light Covers: There is nothing glamorous about a light fitting filled with dead bugs but cleaning one can be tricky because light fittings are all a little bit different. The most common ceiling fittings either use clips to hold the glass in or screws. Lamps are easier, just take out the bulb and unscrew the ring around the light fitting. The last thing you want to do is break the glass and be in trouble with the landlord, so go gently. I always find it easier when I have a friend to pass things to. Make sure the light is off (or lamp is unplugged) and carefully remove the glass. Once you have the glass off, tip out any dead bugs and either hand wash or dish-wash. If the glass is streaky or is not coming clean, wash with a 50/50 white vinegar and warm water mix. Dry the glass properly with a soft cloth and replace the glass.

Extractor and Ducted Air Con Vents: Extractor vents (the kind in the bathroom) and the vents for ducted air conditioning are easy to clean, which is lucky, because if you rent, your landlord is going to want them to sparkle. You'll need a step ladder or ladder so you can reach them and if you don't have a bath or laundry sink, you'll need a watertight tub or bucket big enough to fit the largest vent/fan cover. For the bathroom type vents (you may also find these in kitchens and toilets), just push up a little and twist. The occasional cover will screw in, just unscrew, saving the screws for later. For air con vents, just push up a little and slide them out. I once did this on a too short step ladder and used kitchen tongs to reach that last distance. I don't recommend this but it did work! Once the vents are down, put them in a bath full of warm water, with a good squeeze of dish-washing liquid and couple of cups of vinegar. Let that sit for 30 minutes, give each vent/fan cover a good swish and rinse in warm water. They should be lovely and clean but if there is some residual filth, it should wipe off easily. Dry them well and return them to their place in the ceiling. There is the occasional vent that is impossible to remove. For these, clean them the best you can (dish-washing liquid, warm water, white vinegar) without removing them.

Tip

In a desperate pinch, a flat mop or a broom covered with a cleaning wipe can be used to wipe dust away from high up objects. Be really careful not to knock things around while doing this. It's not a really great solution but if you have only a few minutes before the landlord or visitors knock, it can remove a little grime.

BLINDS AND CURTAINS
Venetians

If the blinds are already relatively clean but dusty, an electrostatic duster used regularly should keep them clean. Another method, depending on your vacuum attachments, is to use the brush attachment on your vacuum cleaner. Once again done regularly is will keep them clean

If your blinds are very dirty it is worth putting the effort in and then maintaining as above.

Really dirty blinds (If they can be removed easily and will fit) can be dipped in a bath of warm soapy water and hung up to dry. Otherwise clean with soapy water by hand.

If the venetians are wooden, put the effort in and polish them with good quality furniture polish (a spray is much easier if you can get a good one). The polish will prevent dust from sticking badly and make maintenance much easier

I've tried every gimmicky product and so far have found them all to be an exercise in futility (not to mention hilarity… picture the neighbours peering in as I'm there standing on a ladder watching my once lovely window covering fall ever so graciously to the floor), and as a word of warning, if you are cleaning metal venetians it is worth wearing cotton gloves under rubber gloves as they can be dangerously sharp.

Roller Blinds

Remove the blinds from the window and arrange them flat on the floor. Carefully vacuum the blind with the brush/upholstery attachment to remove any dust and dirt.

Add the unrolled blinds to a bath half filled with warm water and a little dish-washing liquid and allow them to soak for an hour or two. Use a soft cloth to gently wipe away any marks.

Drain the dirty water and refill with clean water to rinse the blinds. Repeat until all of the soap is rinsed away. Depending on your bathroom, you can rinse the blind under the shower if it can be easily managed.

Arrange the blinds over a clothes airer or outside on a clothesline until they are completely dried. Once clean, just reattach the blind.

Curtains

Curtains can become dusty and quite stale smelling. Not all curtains can or should be washed, so check them for a fabric care label (see Laundry Symbol Guide) and wash or dry clean them accordingly. Otherwise, you can vacuum your curtains by taking them down and vacuuming them. It will really help if you can find a friend to help spread them out while you do it. You can also remove dust and fluff with a clothes brush. To freshen them up you can give them a spritz with a fabric freshening spray such as Febreeze; just test it in an inconspicuous area to be sure that it will not mark.

Shower Curtains

I prefer to buy white fabric (not plastic) shower curtains that can be machine washed and bleached. White always looks clean and makes a bathroom seem bright and airy. I also like white because if the rainbow of hair dyes or brightly-coloured shower gels that I use mark the curtain, I can just bleach it back to white. Check the washing instructions (see Laundry Symbol Guide) on the shower curtain and machine wash with bleach or vinegar as indicated.

UPHOLSTERY AND CARPET CARE

This is an all-purpose oops fixer! It will work on almost anything, even mystery stains. The only stain I treat differently is red wine (red cordial or soda too). Cover a red wine stain in salt, leave overnight to dry completely and vacuum. If the mark remains, continue on with the method below, which can be used on fabrics and upholstery too.

- If the stain is still wet, blot with paper towel or an old towel to remove as much moisture as possible.
- Spray the stain and the edge of the stain with white vinegar. You just want to moisten the stain.
- Cover with a layer of bicarb (about 1 cm (³⁄₈ in) thick) and leave overnight to dry completely
- Vacuum up the bicarb.

This should fix most stains straight up but very wet or bright stains may need a repeat.

Mold or mildew on carpets or upholstery can often be fixed but molds can be dangerous, so please heed the cautionary measures and if you are unsure, consult a professional! Mold or mildew is a sign of damp and sometimes a sign of underlying problems and it will recur if the issue is not fixed.

Start by kit-ing up with rubber gloves and a dust mask before brushing off the 'furry' bits.

Vacuum the area well.

Scrub the area with 1 part water mixed with 1 part rubbing alcohol.

Allow to dry in the sun, if possible, or in a warm, dry, well-ventilated area. If that's not possible a fan, a heater on its lowest setting or a cool hairdryer can be employed.

Stairs and Pet Hair Tip: I am an animal lover but at some times of the year there is more fur on my furniture than on my cats. If you have the same problem, try moistening a rubber glove (the ordinary dish-washing kind) and running it over the couch in one direction. The fur will ball up for easy vacuuming or picking off. Also, an old-fashioned clothes brush is great for your bed and, of course, you! These techniques are great for carpeted stairs or carpeted or upholstered areas that are hard to reach with a vacuum.

CLEANING THE SHOWER, BATH AND TILES

Spray your shower/tiles with undiluted white vinegar; I keep vinegar in an old but clean spray bottle for this. Allow to sit for 30 minutes (or overnight but re mist with vinegar before the next step if it's dried).

Dampen a cloth or sponge and add a teaspoon or so of bicarb and rub over everything. You may need to repeat on any stubborn spots.

It will take a bit of work to get it sparkling but after that, spray with vinegar every day (or often, depending on how much use your shower gets). This will really keep things pretty clean and you can scrub with bicarb as needed.

Cleaning the Grout: If you are using the above cleaning methods you shouldn't have too much need to clean the grout, but if you do, you can scrub the grout with bicarb and white vinegar. If it's really bad (or a huge area) you can use bleach. The best way I've found is to buy a bleach-based toilet cleaner (with the container designed to squirt under the rim of the bowl) to run 'lines' of cleaner on to the grout. Leave for 10-30 minutes and scrub away the mold and dirt.

Cleaning Rust or Blue/Green Drip Marks From Sinks and Tubs: Yes, the answer is white vinegar again! Spray well and leave (if it is awkwardly half way up the side, soak a clean cloth in vinegar and lay over the mark). Dampen a cloth or sponge and add a teaspoon or so of bicarb and rub over everything. You may need to repeat on any stubborn spots.

CLEANING THE TOILET

Spray vinegar on any outside plastic or ceramic and leave for a moment. Wipe over from top to bottom (that is cistern, then lid, then outside of bowl) adding a little bicarb to your cloth to remove any stubborn marks. Continue to clean the inside of the lid, the top and bottom of the seat.

For the bowl, add 225 g (8 oz/1 cup) bicarb, 225 g (8 oz/1 cup) white vinegar and scrub with the brush while fizzing. Wipe over the rim too.

You can also drop a denture cleaning tablet in overnight to keep it sparkly between cleans. Any brand is fine; I just buy the cheapest in the supermarket toothpaste isle.

REMOVING OR REPLACING THE TOILET SEAT

If you have moved into a new place, you may want to remove the seat for cleaning or replace it. Most home/hardware stores will sell replacement seats. Not all seats are the same size/shape or have the same spacing, so be sure to check your old one before you go shopping.

At the back of the seat there may be some tabs that you can flick open, if so open them and unscrew the screw. If not, you will find some plastic nuts coming out of the porcelain at the back of the bowl, unscrew these. You can now clean or replace your seat, ensuring the screws are firmly tightened.

Tap Tip: Run a cloth (or paper towel if you prefer) sprayed with vinegar over the taps to keep them sparkly and mold free.

Tool Tip: Window squeegee and a flat microfibre mop can be great for reaching tricky areas and cleaning walls, etc.

TO CLEAN MOLD AND MILDEW FROM WALLS/CEILINGS/TILES/SHOWER

Wearing rubber gloves, eye protection and face mask (let's not forget that molds can be dangerous) brush off any 'furry' bits.

Spray the area with undiluted white vinegar, I keep vinegar in a spray bottle for this.

Allow to sit for 30 minutes (or overnight but re mist with vinegar before the next step if it's dried).

Dampen a cloth or sponge and add a teaspoon or so of bicarb and rub over everything. You may need to repeat on any stubborn spots.

You can also use a 50/50 bleach and water mix instead of the bicarb and white vinegar or wipe the area with the bleach solution after the bicarb/vinegar method.

Please bear in mind that molds can be caused by poor ventilation or underlying structural issues and if the problem is persistent or very bad you should consult a professional or contact your landlord if renting.

CLEARING DRAINS

I do this every month or so to keep everything clear and have not had a problem yet. It also works once you have a problem with either slow or smelly drains. If this doesn't work for you it is time to call a plumber or the landlord!

- Pour 225 g (8 oz/1 cup) of plain, dry bicarbonate of soda down the drain (if you keep bicarb in the refrigerator to keep smells away you can use it for this rather than throwing it out).
- Get ready with the plug in one hand and pour 1 cup (250 ml/8 fl oz) of white vinegar down the drain. Quickly cover the drain with the plug to avoid a 'mini volcano erupting from the plug. If you spill any bicarb getting it in the drain you can rub it into the sink with a wet sponge to shine up your stainless steel.
- Leave for 30 minutes then pour 1–2 litre (2–3½ pints) of hot water down the drain and voila!
- If you started with a draining problem you may need to repeat.

SPRING CLEAN CHECKLIST

This is the kind of clean a landlord looks for, and if your renting days are over, it's a great annual spring clean list. That said, it's a great list to work through prior to a landlord inspection. Items with ★ should be done more often than annually but I have included them as reminders. Don't forget to check out the chapter on appliance maintenance!

Every Room

- Dust up high including cornices, light fittings and fans.
- Clean air conditioner vents.
- Dust all surfaces.

- Clean the windows and windowsills.
- Wash or wipe any blinds or curtains.
- Vacuum/wash floors.
- Dust baseboards/skirting boards.
- Wipe over electrical outlets and light switches.
- Check doors and walls for grubby finger marks and clean, if needed.
- Wash walls with microfiber flat mop.

Bedrooms
- Clear anything from under the beds and vacuum the floor space.
- Go through wardrobes and drawers and donate or discard anything broken, stained, ill fitting or no longer wanted.
- Clean out bedside tables.

Study/Storage/Laundry
- Clear old papers from your filing system and shred.
- Organise office supplies, throw out pens that don't work and refill any empty supplies such as tape dispensers.
- Organise storage areas.
- Sort and fold linens, and make a list of things that need replacing.
- Clean the iron sole plate and steam mechanism.
- Clean the washing machine (run empty on hot wash with 250 ml (8 fl oz/1 cup) each of bicarb and white vinegar).
- Throw away empty or unused cleaning products and make a replacement list.
- Throw away mop heads, sponges and gloves that are in poor repair and make a replacement list.

Bathroom
- Throw out old medicines (safely, by returning them to the pharmacist), old cosmetics and personal care products and make a list of replacements to be bought.
- Clean or replace toilet brushes and toilet roll holders.
- Replace any sink plugs that are badly worn.
- Wash or replace the shower curtain, if you have one.
- Wash or replace the shower caddy, if you have one.
- Clean mirrors with vinegar and paper towel.
- Clean exhaust fans.

Living Room
- Vacuum upholstered furniture. *

- Clean knick knacks. ★
- Wash removable cushion covers.
- Clean lampshades. ★
- Wipe over framed pictures and clean glass. ★
- Wipe grime from remotes. ★

Kitchen

- Clean the oven and stove top.★
- Clean any exhaust fans and filters.★
- Wash the kitchen bin.★
- Remove spoiled food from the refrigerator and freezer.★
- Wash the refrigerator, inside and out.★
- Clean cupboard fronts.★
- Clean the microwave.★
- Clean and descale the kettle and coffee maker.★
- Polish the sink.★
- Wipe bench/work tops.★
- Clear the pantry of expired items and move items that need using up to the front.★
- Arrange for the cleaning/replacement of water filters and purifiers.★

Catering Know-How

Keeping Cool in the Kitchen

Safety, safety, always safety! As uninteresting as it seems, improper food storage can make you really sick and surprisingly, many people store food items incorrectly. How embarrassing would it be if you took some food along to a bbq, or entertained friends and everyone got sick? Nothing ruins a romantic evening quite like vomiting and diarrhoea. Not only is it easy to store things correctly, but there are some handy charts in this section about how long and where to store food items.

PANTRY STORAGE AND WEEVILS

Tupperware-type containers with airtight seals are the best way to store pantry items. It can take a while to build a good collection, so properly closed snap or zip lock bags can be an effective, low cost option in the meantime. Knowing how long you have had foodstuffs is important too; you can write the date an item was opened directly on the snap/zip lock bags. If you are using a Tupperware-type container, just use a ballpoint pen to write the details on a slip of paper and rest it on top the contents before closing the lid. Apart from things going out of date/stale/off, the biggest threat in the pantry is weevils.

How can you tell if you have weevils in your flour or other dry goods? Look for small black dots in the flour. When fully grown, they will develop wings and you will find them flying around and out of your cupboard! In larval state, weevils will appear as tiny maggot-like worms. Another indicator that weevils have infiltrated your food is the presence of cocoons. Even if you don't see any actual bugs or cocoons, you may see that your flour has formed small clumps that are held together by a sticky string-like substance. This is a sure sign that you've got weevils in your flour.

How to Get Rid of Them

Don't feel bad, most weevils come from items that were contaminated at purchase. If you have them, throw away contaminated food, thoroughly clean any containers with hot soapy water and wash the cupboard too. Add one or two fresh bay leaves to each container or bag. No flavours transfer. You can also keep a few pinned inside your pantry cupboard. However, Tupperware or any plastic container with airtight seals, seals so well you should not have a problem.

REFRIGERATOR STORAGE TIMES

There are plenty of food storage options for items to be kept in the refrigerator; foil, plastic wrap/cling film, Tupperware-type containers and snap/zip locks are all good choices. Most modern, frost-free refrigerators have very dry air, so food storage needs to protect the items as well as keep bacteria from spreading. Raw food and cooked food should be stored separately in the refrigerator. Bacteria from raw food can contaminate cold cooked food, and the bacteria can multiply to dangerous levels if the food is not cooked thoroughly again. Always store raw food in sealed or covered containers at the bottom of the refrigerator. Keep raw foods below cooked foods, to avoid liquid such as meat juices dripping and contaminating the cooked food.

If you intend to store freshly cooked foods in the refrigerator (such as leftover curry), chill it as soon as possible, to avoid bacteria growth but wait until steam has stopped rising from the food before putting it in the refrigerator.

When shopping, buy chilled and frozen foods at the end of your trip and take them home to store as quickly as possible. On hot days, in warm climates, or for trips longer than 30 minutes, try to take an insulated cooler bag or icepack to keep frozen foods cold. Keep hot and cold foods separate while you are travelling.

When you arrive home, put chilled and frozen foods into the refrigerator or freezer immediately. Make sure foods stored in the freezer are frozen hard.

Maintaining the optimum temperature inside a refrigerator is important to minimise the growth of bacteria that can cause food poisoning and spoilage. Set at 0–5°C/32–41°F.

Meat and Dairy Products

Egg, chicken, ham, tuna and macaroni salads: 3–5 days.
Luncheon meats, open package or deli sliced: 3–5 days.
Bacon: 7 days
Sausage, raw — from chicken, turkey, pork, beef: 1–2 days.
Ground beef, turkey, veal, pork, lamb, and mixtures of them: 1–2 days.
Fresh beef, veal, lamb and pork: 3–5 days.
Fresh chicken or turkey: 1–2 days.
Soups and stews: 3–4 days.
Leftover cooked meat or poultry: 3–4 days.
Cooked chicken nuggets or patties: 3–4 days.
Pizza: 3–4 days.

Vegetables

Artichokes: 1 week.
Asparagus: Up to 4 days.
Beans: 4–5 days.
Broccoli: 5 days.

Cabbage: 7–10 days.
Carrots: 2–3 weeks.
Cauliflower: Up to 5 days.
Sweetcorn: 2–3 days.
Cucumbers: 1 week.
Lettuce: 2–5 days.
Mushrooms: 3–4 days.
Bell Peppers/Capsicums: 1 week.
Pumpkin/Butternut Squash – Cut: 5 days.
Radish: 1 week.
Spinach: 2–4 days.
Zucchini/Courgette: 4–5 days.

Fruit
Apples: Up to 4 weeks.
Berries: 2–3 days.
Cherries: Up to 3 days.
Citrus: 2–3 weeks.
Grapes: 3–4 days.
Kiwis: Up to 14 days.
Mangoes: 3 days.
Melons (uncut): 5–10 days.
Melons (cut and in airtight container): Up to 3 days.
Papaya: Up to 7 days.
Peaches and Nectarines: 4–5 days.
Pears: Up to 3 days.
Pineapples: 2–3 days.
Plums: 3–4 days.

Not In the Refrigerator
Vegetables
Onions (kept in a cool, dark place): Up to 2 months.
Potatoes (kept in a cool, dark place): Up to 2 months.
Pumpkin/Butternut Squash: Uncut (kept in a cool, dark place)): Up to 2 months.
Tomatoes: Up to 7 days.

Fruits
Avocados: Up to 5 days.
Bananas: Up to 3 days.

Citrus: Up to 1 week.

FREEZER STORAGE TIMES

The way you defrost food is important too. Just leaving it on the counter can allow a dangerous level of bacteria to grow. There are a few ways to thaw things:

You can place them in the refrigerator 24 hours before you need them. Twenty-four hours should be long enough for a quiche to defrost but something like a large roasting cut of meat may need longer. I like to set defrosting items over a baking tray to catch any drips.

You can use the defrost setting on your microwave. If you are using this method, do it right before cooking and do not refrigerate again until fully cooked.

If you need to quickly defrost a chicken breast or steak, put the chicken or meat in a snap/zip lock bag, make sure it's well sealed with no holes or leaks. Put the bag of chicken or meat in a sink or bowl of cold tap water. You may need to weight it with a can. Change the water every 15–30 minutes or so until defrosted.

Freezer Storage Guide

Luncheon meats, open package or deli sliced: 1–2 months.
Bacon: 1 month.
Sausage, raw, from chicken, turkey, pork, beef: 1–2 months
Ground beef, turkey, veal, pork, lamb, and mixtures of them: 3–4 months.
Fresh beef, veal, lamb and pork: 6–12 months.
Fresh chicken or turkey: 9–12 months.
Soups and stews: 2–3 months.
Leftover cooked meat or poultry: 2-6 months.
Cooked chicken nuggets or patties: Up to 3 months.

Tips

- Not sure the temperature is right? If you are balancing frozen lettuce and melted butter (or even if you're not) refrigerator/freezer thermometers are inexpensive and will ensure you have the right temperature set. Just throw the thermometer in for a few hours and check the results. Check a few areas in your refrigerator, the top and bottom shelves will probably differ but both should be in the safe zone.
- Snap/zip lock bags are perfect for storing things like Bolognese in a flat, space-saving way in the freezer.
- Label what you freeze! Nothing like thinking you have Bolognese when it's actually poached plums!

Kitchen Tools You Need To Own

You don't need every kitchen gadget to cook like a boss. A few good quality tools will have you cooking like a pro. You really don't need every passing fancy. These tools will get you by but if food is your passion, you'll need to venture further. And of course, necessity is the mother of invention. I've improvised over camp fires, made nice meals when the lights were out and cooked a pie in a dog dish! If you have these things, you'll be set to storm your kitchen.

- **2 Litre/1¾ Pint Pot**: If you can, make this heavy-based or Dutch-oven style (a heavy round pot with a lid). Something that goes from the stovetop to oven to table to refrigerator is simply ideal.
- **20 cm/8 in Skillet**: Handy if it can go from the stovetop to oven. Non-stick is also pretty darn handy.
- **4 Litre/7 Pint Stock Pot**: For red or other sauces cooked in volume, as well as soups, stocks and pasta.
- **40 cm/16 in Frying Pan with High Sides**: For risottos, stir fries, and combining pasta and sauce.
- **Strainer (Sieve) and Colander**: Almost the same but colanders with big holes will drain your pasta and the mesh of a strainer will sift flour, remove the pips and pulp from fruits and fix lumpy sauces. You do need both.
- **Masher and Peeler**: It seems so obvious but a masher can be good for making smashed potatoes and a peeler will not only peel but make ribbons of vegetables, which are perfect for salads.
- **Spatula and Whisk**: A decent spatula will be firm but still conform to the bowl. Heat-resistant ones are multi purpose. A whisk can make your lumpy sauce smooth and will be needed for so many cooking tasks.
- **Tongs and Serving Spoons**: Tongs will turn your meat and fluff your salad, they are a great serving tool too. It's almost impossible to serve up with a wooden spoon, so invest in a big ol' serving spoon.
- **Wooden Spoons and Silicone Versions**: You'll need a few of these. I don't favour one over the other but I have quite a few of each. Four kitchen spoons is okay but six or more is lovely. Each type has a role. Wooden spoons can absorb colour and flavour, having a few means not having to use your chilli-making spoon to stir cake batter.

- **Oven Mats/Mats**: I thought they didn't matter. Why have pot holders when a tea towel will do? I have a lovely scar from pulling a chocolate pud from the oven, the tea towel was damp and the heat it conducted caused me to stick my thumb to the ceiling of the oven. While my 19-year-old self yelped, the 30-something me bares the scar!
- **Knives**: A sharp knife causes less chopped fingers than a blunt one. This is where buying the best you can afford really matters. But it's not all about the spend, you can still find some awesome products on the cheap.
- **Chopping Boards**: Plastic boards are not great. If you use them, know that they have a 3-6 month lifespan. A good wooden chopping board is a great investment, as both a board and serving surface.

Kitchen Cleaning Tips

- Clean cutting boards and bench/worktops (not marble though) with undiluted white vinegar before and after use to fight harmful bacteria.
- To clean your sponge or dishcloth, soak it in a mix of white vinegar and hot water for 10 minutes.
- Line cupboards and drawers with pretty paper. It looks cute and catches spills.
- Use plastic tubs to keep things tidy and accessible.

BURNT SAUCEPANS AND CRUSTY CASSEROLES

It happens to the best of us, you walk away and forget about what's on the stove and return to a burnt pan. I once worked with a woman who told me that she used to burn saucepans often and would bury them in the garden so her husband wouldn't find out! All that effort when the solution is easy!

You may need to adjust quantities to suit your pan but add 500 ml (17 fl oz/2 cups) water, 250 ml (8 fl oz/1 cup) white vinegar and 115 g (4 oz/½ cup of bicarbarbonate of soda to the pan and put it back on the heat. Allow the mix to boil gently for a few minutes. While it is heating/boiling, use a wooden or heat safe plastic stirrer to gently scrape off any burnt food.

- Tip out the mix and rinse, if there is quite a lot of burnt gunk, repeat the above.
- If it is really stubborn you can coat the pan base in bicarb, add 250 ml (8 fl oz/1 cup) of vinegar and leave overnight, then move to the next step in the morning.
- To remove the last bits, add a good coating of bicarb and then a splash of white vinegar, and use a sponge to rub off any marks. Rinse well.

I love creamy casseroles, covered in golden, bubbling cheese but I loathe cleaning the dish. Well, I did until I worked this method out. This method works wonderfully for stuck-on food in anything. Like congealed sauces in saucepans, soggy cereal that has adhered to the bowl and dough from mixing bowls.

Fill the offending dish with hot water and a squirt of dish-washing liquid. Let it sit for a few minutes while you attend to other dishes.

Grab a spatula. The kind that is flexible but firm, and made out of thin plastic work the best. More flexible or thicker spatulas are not a match for baked cheese. Use the spatula to scrape the crud off the dish. You may need to tip out the water and refill the dish so that you can see the stuck bits from the floating bits you've scraped off. Once all the chunky bits are dealt with, wash as normal.

It only takes a few seconds and it works a treat. You cannot expect a dishwasher to fix this for you, dish-washing a gunked up thing will only make things harder! I have a dedicated 'dish spatula' by the sink. As the spatula is plastic, it's safe for almost every surface. This also reduces the problem of balled up cheese in scourer sponges (gross). Now you can feel free to cook up a storm without fearing the dishes!

Catering for Everybody

My best friend is allergic to a long list of items (soy, rye, coconut, nuts, seeds) and that means that if she eats them she won't just get sick, she will die. Seriously, she will die. Another friend is so allergic to onions, garlic and things in the allium family that she bleeds from places you'd rather not think of. These are food allergies.

If I eat bananas or honey, I throw up for 12 hours. If my sweetheart eats eggplant/aubergine, his mouth swells and feels gross. That's a food intolerance.

I've been vegetarian all my life. I choose not to eat meat or seafood. My friend is a long-time vegan and eats no animal product. That's a strong ethical decision.

When you entertain others, always ask. I cannot stress enough, Ask! If people have true allergies, you could kill with your menu. Regardless of what you think about others' food issues, it's only right to respect them when you entertain. Always try to meet people's needs by asking, but if you can't meet them be clear on it with them and ask them to advise or bring something. Cook or prepare their food first to avoid contagion and follow the 'crazy allergic' rules below!

Label Love
- Check if the contagion is listed.
- Check for the less obvious names.
- Check it again.
- If something doesn't have a label because it's stored in a container, don't use it.

Crazy Allergic
- Dice your sponge, tea towel or anything you clean with.
- Start with a fresh kitchen, clean with soap and water, drying things well.
- Then spray with alcohol (rubbing or isopropyl), allow to dry.

Cook.

It is important that you are aware that these issues may apply to your guests. It's also important that you understand whether it will kill them, make them sick or that they might just plain not like it. When you have someone in your home, you are responsible. And let's have fun not the ambulance! If you ask your guests in advance if they have any food allergies, and honour their requests there will be lots of fun and it won't end in the emergency room! If you put some thought into your planning, you can keep things safe, happy and fun. Even though it can seem like a bit more work, it's really not much at all. I know that my BFF is always very appreciative and I love to be able to accommodate her. Food with friends is the best!

That said, sometimes you'll have a group of people that just can't find common food ground. I know that with some groups it can be impossible to find something everyone likes. In these times I turn to 'make it yourself' or buffet bar types of meals where each person can add the elements they like and leave off the rest. Think tacos or burritos, personal pizzas, baked potatoes, salad bars and sandwich/sub/panni bars. Even a bbq or grill and a few salads can save the day.

Five Recipes You Need To Know

These five recipes are just the beginning your kitchen mastery. These are the sort of recipes that lend themselves to many, many, variations. Master these and you will have a solid repertoire of dishes. You can vary ingredients based on what you like and what you have on hand. Make a meat-eaters feast or a vegetarian delight. These recipes have earned their place in my kitchen, and I've made them time after time after time.

BASE RISOTTO
Risotto is such a wonderful dish! It's delicate, yet filling and there are endless combinations to be tried. There's a lot of hype about it being difficult but it really couldn't be easier. The key to risotto is having all the ingredients prepared and ready to go before you start. The best risottos do require you to stir almost constantly, which can be quite stress relieving after a hard day! It's also wonderful to have a chat and a glass of wine while you stir. Traditional risottos include a dry white wine but verjuice is a non-alcoholic alternative that keeps well in the refrigerator. If you are serving both meat eaters and vegetarians, cook the whole risotto vegetarian and add meat 'in the bowl' when serving.

Ingredients
85 g/3 oz butter
1 onion, chopped
200 g/7 oz/1 cup arborio rice, rinsed
250 ml/8 fl oz/1 cup white wine
750–1250 ml/1½ pints/3–5 cups hot vegetable, chicken or beef stock
100 g/3½ oz fresh Parmesan, finely grated

Method
1. Add half the butter to a large, high-sided frying pan and set over medium heat. Once the butter is melted, add the onion and cook for 3 minutes till softened.
2. Add the rice and cook, stirring frequently, for 1 minute to coat each grain in butter.
3. Add the wine and stir continuously, until almost totally absorbed.
4. Continue by adding stock ½ ladle at a time, stirring and waiting until it's almost absorbed, before adding the next quantity of liquid. Continue until the rice is well cooked but has a little 'bite' in the middle.

5. Turn off the heat and add the additional butter and Parmesan to taste.
6. Stir through and let it sit covered for 5 minutes before serving. Serve with remaining Parmesan on top.

Quick Notes
A wonderful, easy addition to make a plain risotto sing, is lemon. Add the juice and zest of a lemon at step 5 and be blown away with a Lemon Risotto! It is my favourite risotto and also, the first one I learned to make.

Variations
- Bacon, chopped sausage, chopped chorizo, seafood: Add these at step 1.
- Cooked, diced or shredded chicken: Add this at step 5.
- Cooked pumpkin, beetroot, carrot or other root veg: Add at step 5.
- Smaller florets of broccoli or cauliflower: Add at step 4.
- Diced capsicum (bell pepper), zucchini (courgette), fresh or frozen peas or sweetcorn kernels: Add at step 4.
- Fetta, chilli, capers, olives, soft herbs: Add at step 5.

THE ROUX

A roux is a wonderful thing! It is a cooked slurry of flour and butter. While that doesn't sound appealing, when you add stock it becomes gravy (or a brown sauce) and when you add milk it becomes béchamel (or a white sauce). - They are very similar; let's do a quick gravy first. If vegetarian stock is used, this can be vegetarian.

Ingredients

50 g (1¾ oz) butter
2 tablespoons plain (all-purpose) flour
375 ml (12 fl oz/1½ cups) stock
1 teaspoon Worcestershire sauce
1 teaspoon soy sauce
1 teaspoon Parisienne essence (gravy browning)
Black pepper, to taste

Method

1. Melt the butter in a pan set over high heat and continue until it stops foaming.
2. Add the flour and whisk vigorously to form a roux and cook for a few minutes. You want to cook out that raw flour flavour but you don't want it to colour. This is called a roux.
3. Add the stock while whisking vigorously, to avoid lumps. Continue whisking as the sauce thickens.
4. Add the Worcestershire and soy sauces, gravy browning and seasoning and whisk well before serving.

Variations

If you have roasted some meat and want to make a pan gravy, remove the meat from the pan and drain away a little of the fat from the pan, if it seems excessive. You will be left with a little fat and the brown residue from the roast meat.

Place the roasting dish on the stovetop, over a medium heat. Bring the pan juices to the boil. Add two or three tablespoons of plain (all-purpose) flour and stir until the flour is well combined. Reduce the heat a little and cook, stirring often until the roux is well browned. Make sure you scrape up the tasty meat residue as you stir. Be sure that the roux does not burn. Slowly pour in the stock, stirring constantly until well combined and bring to the boil. Reduce the heat and simmer for about 3 minutes, stirring often. Season to taste.

Béchamel is one of the French mother sauces, which means by making a few tweaks to the recipe it can become a mornay, nantua, mustard, Cheddar cheese, or parsley sauce. It's a fabulous sauce to get acquainted with because it's easy, delicious and super versatile. In fact, there are more variations than I've listed! These sauces really add interest to meat and vegetarian meals, or can even be used as a pasta sauce. If you fancy cooking a moussaka, cauliflower cheese, fish pie, lasagne, mac 'n' cheese, croquettes, or tuna mornay, you'll probably need a béchamel or a variation of it. The recipe here is for a medium consistency sauce because I find it's what I use the most often. If you desire a thicker or thinner sauce see the Quick notes below.

Ingredients
2 tablespoons butters
2 tablespoons plain (all-purpose) flour
250 ml (8 fl oz/1 cup) cold milk
Salt, to taste
Pepper, to taste

Method
1. Melt the butter in a pan set over medium heat and continue heating until it stops foaming.
2. Add the flour and whisk vigorously to form a roux and cook for a few minutes. You want to cook out that raw flour flavour but you don't want it to colour. This is called a roux.
3. Add the cold milk while whisking vigorously, to avoid lumps. Continue whisking as the sauce thickens.
4. Bring the sauce to a boil and add salt and pepper. Continue to cook for 2–3 minutes before removing from the heat.
5. This will make around 250 ml/8 fl oz/1 cup but the recipe can be doubled. If you are cooking the sauce for later use, cover the top with wax paper (touching the sauce) to prevent a skin from forming.

Quick Notes
Thin White Sauce: 1 tablespoon butter, 1 tablespoon plain (all-purpose) flour, 250 ml (8 fl oz/1 cup) milk.

Thick White Sauce: 3 tablespoons butter, 3 tablespoons plain (all-purpose) flour, 250 ml (8 fl oz/1 cup) milk.

Heavy White Sauce: 4 tablespoon butter, 4 tablespoon plain (all-purpose) flour, 250 ml (8 fl oz/1 cup) milk

Variations
Mornay Sauce: Add 60 g (2 oz/½ cup) grated (shredded) cheese to 250 ml (8 fl oz/1 cup) of hot sauce; stir over low heat until the cheese is melted. Season with a little mustard or Worcestershire sauce to taste.

Nantua Sauce: 35 g (1¼ oz/¼ cup) cooked, very finely chopped crayfish, shrimp (prawns), crab or lobster and 1/4 teaspoon hot paprika. Make the béchamel, remove from the heat and whisk in the shellfish and paprika.

Mustard Sauce: Whisk in 2–3 teaspoons prepared mustard after the sauce is thickened.

Cheddar Cheese: Stir in 60–115 g (2–4 oz/½–1 cup) grated (shredded) Cheddar cheese during the last 2 minutes of cooking, along with a pinch of cayenne pepper.

Parsley Sauce: Add 3 tablespoons of finely chopped fresh parsley after the sauce has thickened.

RED PASTA SAUCE

A red pasta sauce is the essence of simplicity but can be so tasty, comfortingly fresh or pungently reduced (that is cooked down to a strong, bold flavour by long, slow simmering) When summer offers up fresh tomatoes and plentiful herbs, something wonderful will come together in moments. But even the dark, depths of winter can be brightened with a sauce made from cans of tomatoes. I was lucky to know an Italian chef; his family still grew their own crops of tomatoes each year, from which they made their tomato sauce. He taught me to be generous with olive oil and salt and add just a little sugar. If the kitchen beckons on a Saturday afternoon, cook up a batch of sauce! It freezes well and when you need comfort, you are only a pot of pasta away...

Ingredients

75 ml (2½ fl oz/¹/₃ cup) olive oil

4 onions, finely chopped

5-6 cloves garlic, minced

125 g/4½ oz tomato paste

1 teaspoon dried oregano

250 ml (8 fl oz/1 cup) water

1 litre (1¾ pints) tomato purée or chopped/crushed canned or 1.5 kg (3¼ lbs) fresh chopped tomatoes, skinned or whole. To skin a tomato, cut a small X in the skin on the stem end, plunge into boiling water for 1 minute. Plunge into cold water and allow to cool. The skin should peel off easily.

2 tablespoons sugar

1 tablespoon salt flakes or 1 teaspoon free-flowing salt

Handful of fresh basil, chopped

Salt and pepper, to taste

Method

1. In a large stockpot and over medium heat, sauté the onions and garlic in the olive oil, until soft and fragrant, about 2 minutes.
2. Add the tomato paste, oregano and any dried herbs, and cook for 2–3 minutes.
3. Add the tomato purée and canned tomatoes, sugar and salt. Stir to mix well.
4. Let the mixture simmer over gentle heat, uncovered, for 2 or more hours (the longer the better, but minimum 2 hours), stirring occasionally.
5. Stir though the basil. Taste for seasoning and season to taste.

Quick Notes

To make Bolognese, add 1.5 kg (3¼ lbs) of minced (ground) meat (beef or beef/pork blend) at step 1, browning and breaking up the meat before proceeding to step 2.

Add fetta, cooked broccoli florets, chopped zucchini (courgettes), or peas to the finished sauce.

Variations

Capers, olives, anchovies – Add at step 3.

Cream – Add 250–500 ml/8–16 fl oz/1–2 cups) at step 5 for a rosé sauce.

Fresh oregano, chilli, chopped roast capsicum (bell pepper) – Add at step 4.

125 CAKE

This cake is lovely and easy, requiring very few tools. A stand or hand mixer makes light work, but a big bowl, wooden spoon and whisk will work just fine. This delicious cake can really be any flavour you want and can be decorated in all manner of ways, including as a single whole cake or as cupcakes. It makes one 20 cm (8 in) round cake, or a neat dozen cupcakes. This recipe can be doubled and two cakes make quite a nice layer cake.

Ingredients
125 g (4½ oz) butter, softened
125 g (4½ oz) caster (superfine) sugar
2 teaspoons vanilla bean paste/extract
2 tablespoons milk
2 eggs
125 g (4½ oz) plain (all-purpose) flour
½ teaspoon bicarbonate of soda (baking soda)
1 teaspoon baking powder

Method
1. Preheat the oven to 180°C/350°F/Gas mark 4. Grease and line 20 cm (8 in) round cake tin (pan) or line a 12-cup muffin pan with paper liners.
2. Cream the butter and sugar in an electric mixer for 3 minutes, or in a large bowl using electric beaters or whisk, until pale and fluffy, about 6 minutes.
3. Add the vanilla, milk and eggs, one at a time and mix by hand until well combined.
4. Combine the flour, bicarb and baking powder in a bowl and add to the batter, sifting it over in two additions, stirring until well combined.
5. Use a spatula to scoop the batter into the cake tin or spoon into the cupcake papers.
6. Bake a whole cake for 40–50 minutes, or until a skewer inserted into the centre comes out clean. Bake cupcakes for 15–20 minutes, or until a skewer inserted into the centre comes out clean.
7. Allow to cool before decorating with buttercream.

Quick Notes:
Don't just think about flavouring the cake itself. You can use a small knife to cut a divot in cupcakes or cut layers into a whole cake that can be filled with jams, jellies, curds, peanut butter, chocolate spread, icing, even little candies or chocolates!

Variations:
Chocolate: Add 2-4 tablespoons unsweetened cocoa powder at step 4.

Chocolate (or cinnamon or butterscotch or whatever chip) chip: Add 85–150 g (3–6 oz/ ½–1 cup) chips and stir in between steps 4 and 5.

Lemon (or orange or lime): Omit the milk, and instead add juice and finely grated zest of a lemon and stir in after step 3.

Mint: This works well with chocolate or choc chip or both. Add ¼–1/2 teaspoon peppermint extract at step 3.

Basic Buttercream

Buttercream is a simple but wonderful icing! It can be simply smoothed over cakes or cupcakes but it can also be piped for a pretty effect and if you are going to get fancy with fondant, it makes a good crumb coat. That popular cupcake swirl (you know the one, it looks a bit like soft serve ice cream) is created by part filling a piping bag fitted with a star nozzle (1M tip from Wilton or the equivalent) with buttercream. Your local cake decorating shop will sell it or you can find it online. It really doesn't take too much time to master with the right tools. This amount of icing will swirl a dozen cupcakes or fill and top a 20 cm (8 in) round cake.

Ingredients

125 g/4½ oz butter, softened OR half butter, half vegetable shortening
250 g/9 oz icing (confectioners') sugar
1 teaspoon vanilla extract (or other extract)
2 tablespoons milk

Method

1. With electric beaters or a mixer, beat all ingredients together in a large bowl for 10 minutes till fluffy. Yes, it takes a while but it's really worth it. Just mixing will not give you the fluffy cloud of sugar sweet you were going for.

Quick Notes

Food colour can really bring the fun to cake making and decorating. Liquid colours are just fine but if you want a very strong colour then using a lot of liquid will thin the icing, so perhaps reduce the volume of milk. Gel colour can really get those brights to pop but a little can go a loooooong way so start with a pin prick size. Butter will always add a little yellow colour, so use your colour theory for the perfect shade. Some people use no butter in their buttercream and only vegetable shortening for this reason but I think the taste suffers. Specialty stores sell clear vanilla if you want to get serious about the final colour being true.

Variations

Chocolate: Add 2–4 tablespoons unsweetened cocoa powder.

Caramel: Omit the milk, add 150 ml (5 fl oz/^{2}/₃ cup) caramel sauce.

Lemon (or orange or lime): Omit the milk, and replace it with the juice of a lemon.

Everything else: You'll be amazed at the array of extracts out there! They can be powerful, so start with a few drops and taste. Repeat until you have your perfect flavour.

BANGING BROWNIES

People will love you for the rich, chocolate goodness that are these brownies. You will be the star of the party, morning tea or other. This recipe wins friends and calms enemies. Even better, you can mix up the dry ingredients and put them in a 1 litre/1¾ pint container and gift them – BAM!

Ingredients

175 g (6 oz/¾ cup) plain (all-purpose) flour
175 g (6 oz/¾ cup) unsweetened cocoa powder
300 g (10½ oz/1½ cups) brown sugar, packed
85 g (3 oz/¾ cup) almond slivers
160g (5½ oz/1 cup) chocolate big buttons (I use dark) or 160g (5½ oz/½ cup) small buttons or chips
3 eggs, lightly beaten
1 teaspoon vanilla extract
250 g (9 oz) butter, melted

Method

1. Preheat the oven to 160°C/325°F/Gas mark 3. Grease and line an 18 x 28 cm (7 x 11 in) slice tin (pan) with baking paper.
2. Add the flour, cocoa, sugar, nuts and chocolate buttons to a large bowl and mix well.
3. Mix in the eggs, vanilla and melted butter.
4. Spoon into baking tray and bake for 30–35 minutes. The result is a crispy crust and fudgey centre!

Great Gatherings

So now you have your place all set up, there might be some entertaining on the cards. Entertaining is definitely the fun stuff. But there might be some not-so-fun stuff when it comes to roommates and neighbours. Either way, I've got you covered.

ENTERTAINING AT HOME

Entertaining is one of the joys of life, but it can be all too stressful if you are trying to impress your boyfriend's parents or a new boyfriend! Not many of us give formal dinner parties with a long list of courses any more. Instead, most people host casual dinners, cocktail parties, and parties for occasions. Trust me, you don't need a party planner to host a wonderful 'do', whatever the occasion.

PLANNING FOR ANY OCCASION

So Fresh and So Clean: A clean and tidy house is a must! For important occasions, spend the week before the event cleaning a little each day. For more casual affairs, make sure the kitchen is clean, whizz the vacuum over the floors and upholstery, and clean the loo.

Spoil the Senses: Fresh flowers, lit scented candles (or spritz of room spray) and mood lighting will set a welcoming tone in any home (see lighting chapter). It's a little way to honour your guests and show them you value them.

A Drink, A Drink, A Drink: It's not all about having enough alcohol to choke a horse. Make sure you have plenty of clean glasses and cups, lots of ice and non-alcoholic drinks for mixers and designated drivers.

HOSTING A DINNER PARTY

Food Glorious Food: I think two or three courses is just right for at-home dining. If you want to amp it up, some nibbles before the first course and/or a post dessert cheese plate will do the trick. Time-honoured recipes that you are comfortable cooking are always the best choice unless you are comfortable getting experimental and don't mind calling for a pizza if disaster strikes – maybe that could be a fun night with close friends but it's probably less than cool if you are out to impress.

Time Is Money: Well, maybe not money in this scenario but you do want to spend time with your guests. It's no fun (and downright rude) to spend the whole night in the kitchen, so plan accordingly. Choose things that can be prepared beforehand and don't take too much time to finish off. Or, have two prepared dishes and only one that will take you away for a while. Or, invite your guests into the kitchen to chat while you stir a risotto, or involve them in the cooking by getting them to top their own personal pizzas or serve themselves with a baked potato bar.

Musical Chairs: If you have a dining room setting that will accommodate everyone for a sit down meal, great! But if you have to drag in chairs, always seat yourself in the worst one and make closer friends (or housemates or boyfriends etc) sit in the next worst one, saving the best for the most honoured of your guests. If a table setting isn't an option, eating on your lap can be an option but plan foods that can be eaten with just a fork or spoon to avoid awkwardness!

Chocolate Fixes Everything: If you are a less than amazing cook or are buying in most of dinner, wow them with dessert! Who doesn't love dessert? Plus, as the last course, it will be fresh in their minds.

Ladies First: Even at more casual affairs, observing the time-honoured traditions of dining etiquette has a certain charm and will signal that you know what you are doing to any guests that know these social codes. Anyone accustomed to fine dining and expecially the older generations will enjoy and respect your efforts. Always serve the most important/hounoured guests first, then go down the order, with hosts coming last. When you are serving food at the dining table, stand at the person's left as you put down the plate and remove the empty plate from the right.

DINNER TABLE DON'TS

These rules are not necessary in every situation but better to be kept in mind when you are dining in someone else's house or find yourself somewhere upscale.

- Don't make a fuss. If you don't like something, leave it. If you take a mouthful and it contains something you cannot swallow, you should excuse yourself and remove it in privacy. Absolutely do not do so at the table and never place it in your napkin or on your plate for all to see.
- Don't blow on hot food to cool it down. Wait for it to cool itself.
- Don't photograph the table, it looks tasteless, desperate and screams fine dining novice.
- Don't expect the waiting staff to be psychic. If you are finished but have food on your plate, place the knife and fork together on the plate and sit back from the table a little.
- Don't move your plate after your meal has been served.
- Don't treat the waiting staff poorly. It makes you look common rather than in control.
- Don't eat chicken or chops with your fingers.

- Don't point with your cutlery.
- Don't hold your fork while you drink your wine.
- Don't overstay your welcome. You can see a restaurant is getting ready to close. If you are in someone's home and offer to leave, their response will tell you if they honestly want you to stay.
- Don't discuss politics, religion, or sex at the table, unless you know every guest very well. You should also avoid any controversial subjects that may fall outside of the scope of those three topics. Dinner is meant to be enjoyed, not to be a forum for debate.
- Don't talk only to the person seated to one side of you. Share your conversation with the person to your left and to the right.
- Don't take a small pre-dinner snack from the serving tray and put it straight in your mouth. They must always touch your plate (or napkin if no plate has been provided) before being put in the mouth.
- Don't start eating until everyone has been served. If there are a large number of guests, the host/s may indicate that you may begin before everyone is served. If this is the case, you should begin
- Don't smoke at the table or anywhere unless invited to do so by the host/s.

Tip

In a buffet, serve-yourself-style situation, FHB (Family Hold Back) applies. Let your guests have the pick of the choicest cuts and serve themselves first before you dig in.

BE THE BEST GUEST

When someone invites you to their occasion, you can't just eat, drink and leave! Always ask the host/s if there is anything you can bring and make sure you bring what was requested. Even if they say they need nothing, bring flowers, wine or chocolates to thank them for their hospitality. Be on time but be apologetic if the host/s isn't ready. Always ask if you can help with preparations and after all is said and done, offer to help with the dishes. Send the host/s a text or email the following day to thank them for having you. Be sure to return the compliment and invite them over to your home too.

Budget Entertaining Tips
- Ask each person to contribute a course
- Pick brunch, breakfast or afternoon tea
- Provide cheese and snacks and ask others to bring the wine

Gifts, Birthdays and Occasions

There are times in life where it seems like there is a birthday or wedding every weekend. Life is busy, the budget is tight and it can be hard to find the time or cash to deal with all those occasions. Too often, my partner has informed me of a party invite and forgotten to tell me it was actually a birthday or house warming until we were about to leave our house! I didn't want to look like I didn't care but what to do at the last minute?

CREATE A GIFT TUB
Stock your tub well and you can be party prepared in minutes flat! It might seem boring but it saves last minute panic. Keep these things together and regardless of the holiday (Christmas, Mother's or Father's Day) or celebration, you'll be covered.

Paper Plains: Keep some gender neutral, plan wrapping paper on hand – silver, gold, black, white or brown craft paper work well. Add a stash of white tissue paper for safe packaging and filling out boxes, bags and baskets.

Packages Tied Up With String: You'll need to wrap gifts with flair too. Wrapping ribbons (gold and silver are always elegant), fabric ribbons, string or yarn are good to keep in stock. And don't forget ribbon rosettes, pom poms or other embellishments.

Keeping Up With Cards: It's always handy to have a range of birthday cards that cover both genders, some housewarming ones and Christmas, Mother's or Father's Day cards. Add in anything that seems to be happening a lot right now – engagement, marriage, baby, etc.

The Usual Suspects: Tape, scissors, nice pen or marker. Trust me, you won't be able to find them when you need them. These items are a special breed of creature that hide at the least appropriate moments!

Guilty Gifts: It pays to have a few all-purpose gifts on hand such as cute kitchen items, accessories and gift cards. If Aunt Mavis gave you necklace and earring set that is beautiful but just not you, throw it in there too but make sure you keep a note with it saying who gave it to you. The trick to successful re gifting is that the original gifter must never find out and the person you give it too must not know it was re gifted. So if you posted pics on Instagram when you received it, you are dead in the water now!

Tag Tip: Get some cool, all occasion addressing tags. That way if you're not 100 per cent sure of the occasion, you aren't giving a birthday card at a housewarming!

DRESS CODES DECODED
Nothing has the power to turn me into a babbling mess than the term 'smart casual'! Too casual and you look sloppy, too dressy and you look a try hard who didn't get the memo. In fact, that's the issue with all dress codes, isn't it? But don't panic, I've cracked the code and created this neat guide.

White Tie
The most formal of dress codes and the dress of fancy balls and even fancier weddings. Dresses must be floor length, either evening gowns or ball dresses. Long gloves and lashings of bling are required. A tailcoat, hat and white bow tie will be expected of men.

Black Tie
A popular choice for fancy weddings and award ceremonies. Dresses should be long evening gowns. This is your chance to bring that old Hollywood glamour with light-catching satin, sequins and beads. Men should be looking dapper in a Tuxedo with either the trad black bow tie or the modern skinny black tie.

Formal or Black Tie Optional
This a confusing one. Ladies should keep to the rules of black tie. Long dresses are still the only choice. A tux is still a fitting choice, but if they choose, men get to step it down a notch and wear a dark suit and tie.

Lounge Suit, Cocktail or After 5
This is one that will absolutely come up from time to time. The ladies get to show a little leg in knee length dresses. Keep it classy though! Not too short, not too tight, not made of stretchy fabric. This is still an evening wear event, dress code wise, even if you are attending a wedding in the day. Men can wear an appropriate suit and tie but a dark suit is always a little more dapper.

Smart Casual
Ah, my dress code nemesis! Popular for casual or beach weddings and for occasions such as daytime work events. The 'casual' part does not mean jeans, not for anyone, not ever! What it does mean is dressy sun dresses, pants or skirts with a blouse and blazer or if the event is in the evening, wear dresses that are a touch too simple to be 'cocktail'. Men should stick to pants and a shirt or a restrained suit.

Regardless of the level of dress code, you can be sure these things apply:

- Choose an outfit that enhances your legs or bust. Not both together, that is just vulgar. A wrap or cardigan or shrug can minimize the display of flesh for both arms and bust.
- Shoes should be in good condition and clean. If you can't walk elegantly in evening wear shoes them choose something else. You don't want to look like a foal finding its feet. Smart casual never means trainers.
- Never wear black or white to a wedding, unless you have been specifically asked to.
- Never, under any circumstance, wear tights or stockings with open toe shoes.
- Neat, clean fingernails are a must for both sexes so treat yourself to a manicure (and pedicure if you have open shoes).
- Choose long wearing makeup and easy-fix lip products for formal occasions. After all a clutch bag only has so much space.
- Let one part of your look shine. Vampy makeup and nails paired with a racy dress, dangerous stilettos and bring-it-on hair is too much in one look. Choose the focus, amp it up and let the rest be more sedate.
- The right underwear will make a world of difference to how you look and feel. A gown will glide over the right underpinnings. ?Hitching up your bra all night will look awful and draw attention to yourself. ou must feel comfortable in what you wear, even if you are a mile from your comfort zone. Stand up straight, stop adjusting yourself and focus on being witty and engaging!

Social Situations

Noisy Neighbours

Apartment or close living can equal the potential to have noisy neighbours. There's regular noisy stuff such as vacuum cleaners, clunking washing cycles, lawn mowers and all the other sounds of life. And then there's loud music, raucous parties, arguing couples and yelled mobile conversations, right by your open windows. There is nothing appealing about trying to sleep while a neighbour is playing music loud enough to wake the dead! But what to do about it?

Start by soundproofing your space. If you are renting, you probably can't cover your walls in soundproofing foam (nor would you want to!) but there are a few tricks you can try:

Soft furnishings can help absorb sound, so adding rugs to floors will help if you have noise below you. It will also reduce the noise your downstairs neighbour hears from you.

Hanging rugs, quilts and fabric wall hangings can reduce sounds from the other side of the wall. Fabric covered corkboards can help too and can be part of the décor. Even a curtain and curtain rod can look good.

If sound is coming from across the hall, make sure you have a weather strip or a draught-excluding snake covering any gaps below the door.

If you have sound from outside, heavy curtains can help.

Try to drown it out, I'm not suggesting cranking up the stereo, something more subtle may do the trick. Quiet background music can sometimes cover the noise. Or, try white noise such as a fan, white noise recording or app. Listening to something using headphones can get you through the occasional bout of noise.

If none of these tricks work and the problem is ongoing, you will have to approach the offending neighbour. Here are some hints for approaching the sound issue.

Don't Threaten Drastic Action Straight Up, It Could Backfire: A neighbour once called the police about my stereo volume, rather than asking me to turn it down. The police attended and found my noise level acceptable. I offered to turn it down but they told me I was fine. I'm sure my neighbour was none too pleased but it's worth noting that one person's too loud is another's acceptable. Plus, I would have turned it down if I'd been asked nicely.

Passive Aggressive Is, Well, Passive Aggressive: Don't waste your energy renaming your wifi connection to 'death to noisy neighbours'. The probably won't see it and if they do they may just up the ante. Nasty notes and notices left in common areas of the building or thumping on the walls are just as likely to start a war. The same goes for veiled threats, profanity and name calling.

Take In the Neighbourhood: If you are living among a bunch of student neighbours, the noise of a party might not even be noticed, but if you have a family next door, a loud tv could cause offense. If you are new to the neighbourhood, try and get a feel for it before taking action. If your noise issues are short term, as in you are studying for a big exam or working night shift for a month, don't be scared to ask for a temporary hush. Explain to your neighbours and they may be happy to help.

Convenient Compromise: A friend lived in a group of flats where the weekends meant music from Friday afternoon to Sunday night. Her neighbours shared similar musical taste and decided on 'special knock'. If they preferred her musical picks, they would knock on the wall with the special knock. She would turn up her stereo and they would turn off theirs and vice versa. No doubt, this is somewhat rare but it is a very cool thing if it works.

It's a matter of timing. A friend of mine had a noisy neighbour who played music from 5 pm to 1 am. She asked her neighbour if they could tone it down after 10.30 pm. She didn't mind hearing the daily music but got up early for work. Her neighbour was more than happy to keep it down in the later hours.

Negotiating With Terrorists: If you come with options on how the noise issue can be fixed, you'll be more likely to get a satisfactory result. No one likes to be told off, so approaching things in a collaborative way can reduce the confrontation factor. If you are dead set on a certain point, try giving them choices about how they can do that for you. No one likes to be backed into a corner or feel like they cannot do as they choose in their own homes. Giving options allows people to feel that they resolved the issue and less like they gave in to a demand.

Waiting is the Hardest Part: Don't run off to chat to your neighbour the first time they are loud. Give it time to see if it is a rare thing or a common occurrence.

If they scare you… or you are unsure about knocking on their door, go to see the neighbours with a friend. The old, safety in numbers thing is good but use the technique to your advantage. If you are obviously video or sound recording the interaction, you will make things much worse but a hidden voice recording is a handy backup if it goes to hell.

What to do if you've paid your neighbour a visit and it didn't go well? If they behave in an abusive or threatening manner, then remain polite and calm. Politely end the conversation and walk away. Then you may want to think about reporting them. Same goes if they ignore you.

If you have no luck with speaking to them directly, you can try contacting your landlord or the local council to report the situation. In fact, there are some situations you should report. Barking dogs can be the cause of noise complaints but a dog regularly and consistently barking or yelping may be in distress. If the dog is being mistreated, reporting it will let the authorities know. If it is a simple separation anxiety on the dog's part, the neighbour may not be aware of it and reporting will let them know.

If you hear an argument that is more than an argument, or if you think someone is in danger, a call to the police is a good idea especially if children are involved. I've had the unfortunate experience of contacting the police about this. At one time, my downstairs neighbours engaged in regular fights but one sounded very physical and was accompanied by sounds of breaking glass and very chillingly, a child's shrill plea for daddy not to hurt mummy. I won't lie, it was scary to call the police each time they fought to extreme, and I feared some sort of retaliation. But I'm glad I did because after that terrifying fight he was arrested and she moved interstate with her child. I like to think I played a small part in helping them dodge a bullet.

Make sure you are being a good neighbour.

If you are being noisy, try and keep it within reasonable hours, no earlier than 8 am and no later than 9-10 pm. Up to midnight is reasonable on weekends. To be sure you are keeping on the right side of things, call your local police station or council to check the laws and guidelines for where you live. Knowing your legal obligations will make any complaints easier to handle.

If you are hosting a party, slip a note to your neighbours a week before to let them know. Invite them, if you like, but make sure that you make it clear that they can ask you to tone it down if it gets too loud for them. Most people will be cool about it if they have some warning.

Be mindful of open doors and windows and close them if you are being loud.

If a neighbour approaches you about the noise, ask them what times are best for them and which noises are the issue. Be polite and turn it down.

Remember, if you can hear them, chances are they can hear you!

Top Tip

The advice and common sense in this section should also apply to the care and control of communal areas, such as stairwells, landings, laundries, garbage areas, gardens and car parks. Don't be a dick to your neighbours and approach them sensibly when what they do is annoying!

Living Alone Or With Roommates

However you choose to live, with people or solo, it can get tough! Living with others will always come with hazards, their personality, lifestyle or toenail clippings! When you live with others you not only share a house, in some ways you share your life. The best way to keep a shared space from turning sour, is to start it off well. If you are planning on living with others, consider these things first:

Rights and Responsibilities Rule, OK? Know what you are signing up for when you sign anything. Bills in your sole name are your responsibility legally, regardless of who owes what. Just because something is in joint name doesn't get you off the hook. Most joint financial agreements (bills, leases, mortgages, etc) are 'jointly and severally liable', meaning that if the other person takes off, you may be liable for the whole bill. It's really worth knowing what your responsibilities are and what rights you have if other parties don't do their bit.

Oh, There's Got To Be Guidelines. Before you make living arrangements (whether they are moving in with you or you with them) work out what the guidelines are. Think about food, privacy, internet use, late nights, early mornings, parties and, of course, all things financial. A while back, I was part of a shared house. Two people worked 9–5, one worked all sorts of shifts and one hospitality hours. I would be woken by my hospitality friend having drinks and cheese with friends at 3 am. Not fun before an early meeting at work, but the cheap, high end champagne softened the blow! You also have to know if you are okay with a housemate's one night stand using your conditioner before you make the deal. You don't want to be stuck doing the dishes (like the only one who does the dishes) before you can make yourself dinner. Work that stuff out before the reality sets in.

I Think It's Called Common Courtesy. If the only other people you've lived with were related to you, you might want to read this section carefully. Not everyone has the same tolerances, wants, needs, desires and morals. If you're not sure what I mean answer this question: Is it okay to pee with the door open? Whatever your reaction, I bet it was strong. I also bet someone else would have a different reaction. That's what I want to capture; everyone is different and courtesy will ease the difference. Some guidelines and things to think about are:

• If you didn't buy it, don't eat or drink it.

- And that goes for, if it's not yours, don't touch it.
- You break it you buy the replacement.
- You wreck it, you replace it.
- You didn't pay for it, it's not yours.
- You mess it, you clean it.

If you have set your guidelines, this stuff shouldn't come up much but maybe it has to be said. You have to consider the lives that the people you live with are having. It's a jerk move to be loud when a housemate has a big deal in the morning, or to give someone a hard time while they are stressed, sick or trying to recover from a break up. If you are in doubt, think about how you would want others to behave toward you if you were in their situation. That is, and always will be, one of the best ways to work with other people. If you aren't sure what to be, be kind.

Documentation Wins the Day: Stupidly easy as a thought but harder in practice. Keep a copy of anything you sign. But more than that, back it up! Of course, I mean back it up digitally. Be aware that a document is not the whole story. I've always taken comprehensive pictures of anywhere I've moved into, showing any existing damage and current condition. In many cases a simple photograph is not enough for a landlord, tribunal or court, they must be dated verifiably. I suggest sending them via email to a friend or setting up a new email address and emailing the photos to it with any descriptions needed. In my experience, sending to a third party has been best. This applies to issues of room mates too. Photographic, video or audio can help prove your case in situations of dire need. Need I say, uploading that to YouTube, soundcloud or whatever, is just passive aggressive and will come to no good! When you choose to live alone there is that glorious buzz (Barbra Streisand's *All By Myself* playing as you turn circles til you're dizzy) and then somewhere a little thud as you realise that this whole thing is your responsibility and you're kind of lonely. I believe that living alone and working how you tick is the coolest thing you can ever do. It can be sudden shock though. Living alone has its own considerations, and it's not for everyone. Like many things, if you're not ready for it, you may be ill prepared. Here are some thoughts, considerations and little tricks to help your solo life be sensational.

The Loud Sound of Silence: Music, TV or white noise running in the background can make things feel more familiar, if that's what you crave.

Social Planner: On your own you can get sucked into your own space and not want to come out or feel the other way, alone and left out. Be careful not to isolate yourself. Make some plans with your mates.

Phone Friends: Sometimes a quick text or call will help when there is no one to hear how your day went. If you don't make arrangements to phone or text people, you might feel like you are bothering them. And sometimes you just need to share!

Dine Fine: If there is no one to share a meal with you might get into a habit of not bothering to cook properly and eating toast for dinner instead. There are lots of books on cooking for one or two; it's not all about freezing for later. Don't stop enjoying food, it's one of life's delights!

Plucky Pets: If you are allowed them, pets make wonderful company. They don't care if you talk to them or sing off key: Ask my cats!

No One Messes With Me: If you are on your own, you'll never wake up to a mess you didn't make! But you know who made the ones that you have!

Feel Free: If you want to eat yogurt, while wearing a face mask, and sporting your holey old sweats, while watching *Dirty Dancing* again…the whole house is your oyster!

So, whether you live alone or with others, remember it's your life – live it with responsibility and flair. Don't scrimp on the generosities you pay others or yourself but never be a doormat. Also, remember where you live is a reflection of you. And don't fret if what you have is less than lustrous; we all started out somewhere, only to end up somewhere else. There are so many joys in every house, sometimes you don't even realise what they are until you have left. Savour every house experience, you may never have another like it! Unless you have a sizable trust fund, you are going to have to learn as you roll through different housing situations before you find what works for you. And I wish you the wisdom of these pages and a little godspeed as you get there!

Serious Stuff

Car Maintenance

A car is a big investment, even if yours is an old, second-hand clanger. Just like anything else, a bit of maintenance can save you big bucks and big trouble in the end. Regular servicing and the replacement of tyres and wiper blades and, of course, a good clean every now and then are crucial. It's good to be prepared for emergency situations of all kinds.

THE IMPORTANCE OF EMERGENCY MOTOR ASSOCIATIONS

Almost every country has some sort of membership organization that will provide emergency roadside assistance for dead batteries and flat tyres among other things. I think they are absolutely worth every cent. There is nothing more terrifying than being stuck on the side of the road (in the middle of nowhere or worse, in a busy intersection) alone, and in the middle of the night. And, it is never fun to hear your car make a pitiful click, rather than roaring into life on a busy weekday morning. That's when emergency roadside assistance is wonderful. Not only will it come to you, providing expert help, but the associations are served by professionals you can trust. It really is a matter of safety. There is no guarantee that a passing stranger will offer assistance and there is no guarantee that the stranger who stops is not an axe murderer. Also, without emergency lights/cones/high visibility vests, you could be in danger while working on your car while it is at the side of the road. Plenty of people have been hit doing just that. So, do yourself a favour and get a membership! If you regularly drive in the country or long distances, be sure to investigate what your membership covers and upgrade if there is a better deal for the driving you do.

NOT ALL EMERGENCIES ARE MECHANICAL

Some people just use their cars to get to and from work, others almost live in them. There was a time when I lived between my own place and my now husband's. Our houses were a good hour apart, worse in peak hour and it was sensible to have a small collection of clothes and shoes in my car. I have a list of things that are handy to keep in your car. I think some are non-negotiable and others are about what fits your lifestyle. Either way they may just get you out of sticky situations!

You'll Definitely Want:
- Jumper cables/jump leads – Handy if you need to jump start your car or someone else does.

- Coolant/anti-freeze: Whichever applies to where you live.
- Water: For drinking in an emergency and for overheating emergencies. Also handy for dealing with messes.
- First aid kit: Better safe than sorry, right?
- Tissues and/or baby wipes: For all the usual uses, but handy if you need to use a bathroom that doesn't have any toilet paper, as well as mop up a spill or fix your makeup.
- Bin bags: For rubbish, containing messes, and for use as an ugly but helpful carrier bag.

Maybe You'll Want:
- Spare coat/parka/jacket: For those times when you are freezing or if you are stuck on the side of the road without the luxury of a car heater.
- Spare knickers: For period emergencies and impromptu sleep overs.
- Condoms/tampons/pads: It goes without saying!
- Spare outfit: Great when spending time across two houses.
- Spare shoes: It's always handy to have flats when heels get too hard and if you are keeping an outfit on hand, you'll want the shoes for that too.

HOW TO CHANGE A TYRE

Maybe you didn't heed my emergency motoring association advice, maybe you just want to do it yourself, or maybe you like to be prepared. Before I was allowed to drive a car, I was taught how to jump a battery, change a tyre, fill a tyre with air, fill the radiator and check the oil. These are very cool things to be able to do. Even if someone else is doing them, you can understand what's happening. Learn them if you are interested. To change a tyre:

Secure the Vehicle So That It Won't Roll: Never change a tyre on an incline or hill. Always try to find a flat area, even if it means driving on a flat tyre for a short distance. Use bricks, wooden wedges or metal wheel chocks to block the wheels at the opposite end of the car from the end that is to be raised. Roll the spare tyre to the scene of the action. Pry off the wheel cover. You can use a screwdriver to pry the wheel cover off. Just insert the point of the tool where the edge of the cover meets the wheel, and apply a little leverage. The cap should pop off. You may have to do this in a couple of places, as if you were prying the lid off a can of paint. Go gently, you don't want to damage the car or yourself. Always aim away from your body and other people, knife safety rules apply to screwdrivers too.

Loosen the Lug Nuts: Find the end of the wrench that fits the lug nuts on your vehicle, and fit it onto the first nut. Apply all your weight to the bar on the left. This starts turning the nut anti (counter) clockwise, which loosens it. Don't remove the lug nuts completely, just get them loose enough to remove by hand after you jack up the vehicle. If you have alloy wheels that are held on by lug nuts with delicate finishes, the delicate aluminium or chrome-plated lug nuts need careful handling. They should never be loosened or replaced with power tools that can scratch the delicate finish.

Place the Jack Securely Under the Edge of the Car: Proper locations may vary among vehicle models, so consult the owner's manual for the right places to put the jack. Jack up the vehicle about 20 cm/8 in off the ground.

If You Have a Scissor Jack: insert the rod or wrench over the knob and then crank. If you have a hydraulic jack place the handle into the appropriate location and pump up and down. Use nice, even strokes, taking the jack handle from its lowest point to its highest point on each stroke to cut down on the labour involved.

Take the Lug Nuts Completely Off By Hand and put them in a safe place — inside the wheel cover or hub cap works well. Grasp the flat tyre with both hands and pull it straight toward you. As you pull the flat tyre off, it should slide along the bolts until it clears the end of the bolts and you'll find yourself supporting its full weight. Roll the flat tyre along the ground to the rear of the vehicle to get it out of the way.

Lift the spare onto the lug bolts: Because tyres are heavy, you may have a little trouble lifting the spare into place — especially if you're not accustomed to lifting heavy things. Replace the lug nuts and tighten them by hand. Give each lug nut a jolt with the wrench to get it firmly into place but wait until the car is on the ground before you really try to tighten the lug nuts. After the vehicle is resting on the ground, use the lug wrench to tighten the lug nuts as much as you can.

Replace the Wheel Cover or Hubcap: If your car has wheel covers with a delicate finish, the owner's manual should provide instructions for replacing it. If your car has hubcaps, place the hubcap against the wheel and whack it into place with the heel of your hand. Cushion your hand with a soft rag first so that you won't hurt it. And don't hit the hubcap with a wrench or hammer or you'll dent it. Even if your spare is fully inflated, check the pressure at the next possible opportunity.

Moving House and Changing Address

Oh how I've been there and done that! I swear I am semi-professional at moving house now. Not only have I moved many times, I've helped friends move too. I've gone the DIY way, with rented trailers, horse floats and vans and I've also had the pros in once or twice. It seems the older you get, the more stuff you have, the more people you have to let know and the harder it seems. This guide is the compiled advice of 20-something nomadic renters!

DATES AND TIMES, PEOPLE AND PLACES

Once you have your moving dates, it's all about people. That is arranging the real estate, the movers (paid or friends), anyone you'll live with and of course, yourself. It is a wonderful thing to have some time overlap so you can have access to both properties at one time. Of course, that can leave you paying two rents for a little while. You need to have time to move out of the old place and clean it up, while simultaneously setting up the new place. If the crossover is very tight (such as a day or two), find a friend to help with a bed for a few nights. That way you can shove your stuff in the new place and not worry about making it functional while you clean out the last place.

If you are opting for the DIY version of moving, you'll need some friends. Ask nicely and realise they'll probably ask you to help next time they move and really, you'll have to do it. It's only right! Be prepared to stand the cost of pizza and beers at the end of the day for everyone too. You'll need at least one large trailer (covered if there is the slightest hint of rain)/truck/ van. You'll need a car to pull the trailer and driver capable and confident to pull it. A few regular cars can be more helpful than you'd think. Of course, paying petrol is a must.

I've had such great help from friends and family on moving day. I once moved my stuff from my house, my partner's stuff from his house, stuff from my storage unit and some big appliances from his mum's place all on the same day. We started at 8 am with helpers organised into teams. My mum and gran positioned at the new house, cleaned and unpacked. A male friend and my boyfriend had a big horse trailer and made three drops of boxes, furniture and appliances to the new home. My BFF and I each made three trips in our separate cars of stuff that mostly never got packed, and awkward items such as big vases of faux flowers, as well as makeup and bits. By 9 pm everything was unpacked, lamps were plugged in and throw cushions scattered! Eight people worked like crazy for 12 or so hours. Miracles can happen but you really must organise like clockwork. Further down, I'll talk you through the plan for the day and hopefully you'll experience moving miracles too!

Now that you have the times, dates and people to help you, it's time to organise your paperwork. You'll need to notify significant people of your change of address. A mass email or text will sort out your mates but there's a dizzying array of organizations that need to know too. The handy list below covers almost everybody. Check it out and be sure to let these companies and services know. You may be able to set up a mail forwarding service via the post office; these often cost but can be a massive help if you move quickly and didn't get a chance to change everything over before the move. There is also the matter of setting up and shutting off utilities but we will get there in a moment.

CHANGE OF ADDRESS CHECKLIST

- Your employer
- Electric
- Gas
- Water
- Garbage/Rubbish
- Telephone/Mobile
- Cable
- Internet
- Water Delivery / Water Treatment
- Pool Services
- Lawn / Garden Services
- House-cleaning Services
- Doctor / Veterinarian
- Attorney /Lawyer
- Banks
- Loan Institutions
- Major Credit Card Companies
- Department Store Credit Cards
- Insurance Agencies (Health, Home/Life and Auto)
- Charge Accounts
- Pension Plans/Superannuation
- Air Miles Rewards Program
- Accountant / Tax Consultant
- Professional Memberships / Licensing Boards
- Post Office
- Veteran Affairs
- Income Tax /IRS
- Family Support/Social Security/Pension Benefits/Unemployment

- Vehicle Registration
- Driving Licence
- Subscriptions, inc subscription boxes
- Newspapers
- Magazines
- Mail Order Houses

MAY THE POWER BE WITH YOU

You are going to need electricity and gas, water, telephone or internet immediately that you move. Your lease or rental agreement should state what is included and if you are at all unsure of what you will need to arrange for yourself, then ask! As soon as you know the moving dates, call your energy provider to arrange connection at the new place and disconnection at the old. It is wise to pay a couple of extra days on each end. Say I'm moving out on the 2nd of the month but my lease ends on the 5th, I would arrange disconnection for the 6th. That way I can be assured of power (and other services) while I clean and until I've handed back the keys. Important to note, if the house has an alarm requiring power and you cut the power before your tenancy ends, you could get blamed in the event of a break in! So, moving on with the example, I would start power to the new house as at the 1st, or earlier if my tenancy begins earlier. That way, from the day I take on the new lease, I can start to clean or move in.

If you are moving over a weekend, this stuff is even more important! My BFF moved in over a long weekend. She had organised the electricity connection to start on Friday but didn't check it till she moved in on Saturday. Guess what? No electricity till Tuesday. With two small children, she had to go and stay with her folks till the power was on. Make sure you have this 100 per cent sorted before the move.

If you have left a trail of unpaid bills, don't think it won't catch up! If your credit is in tatters, it might be difficult to get utilities to agree to supply you! It can be easy to freak out and ask someone else to put it in their name but be honest with yourself and them. Maybe this is the universe telling you that this move will come to no good. Also, don't think you can get away with not paying the last bill at the old place because, hey you're disconnected, what can they do? That's asking for trouble. If you are having trouble with cash flow while you are ending and beginning, negotiate with your creditors.

PLAN THE PACK

As early as possible, get boxes! Speak to your local supermarket, alcohol shop or local deli/grocery store/convenience shop/bodega/off-licence and ask if you can have boxes. They will tell you the best time to call to collect any and may even set some aside for you. Get a couple of rolls of good quality, wide packing tape. Don't scrimp on tape; you don't want the bottoms to fall out of your boxes. Grab a handful of markers or sharpies and an A5 pad or some printer paper. Some newspaper is very handy too.

Pack the things you won't need immediately now such as books, CDs and DVDs. Pack heavy items in smaller boxes so that the boxes are liftable. Use the paper to label the box with its designated room and the box contents, then tape it to the box. That will help give the people moving you an idea of where to put stuff if you're not there and you'll know what's in a box at a glance.

Think about hiring a skip or find out about the opening hours of your local dump. Trust me, NEVER move things you could have thrown out first. If you have furniture or other items that won't be coming with you, list them for sale online, in the paper or on community boards. You don't want things happening at the last minute – you just don't need the stress.

Logistical Issues

Are you sure that all of your furniture and appliances will fit into the space you are moving into? Not just the inside spaces but will they make it through doors, up staircases and into position? Now is the time to find out. If you are DIY moving, how will the heavy or big things get onto the transport? Do you have tons of friends or even better a sack truck/dolly/hand truck? I have found them invaluable and cheap to rent or even better, borrow. I once had to walk into a crowded pub and yell out that I needed four guys to lift my refrigerator and promise two pints each in return! Not a good look, so plan the logistics first.

OMG I'm Outta Here

As moving day looms closer, it's so easy to think that packing everything in a fit or frenzy is a good idea. Slow your roll a little and think about the actual moving day. When I move (or run a festival or event) I have 'The Box Of All Things'. This box contains what you need, right when you need it. It contains the last things to be packed and the first things on the scene at the new place. Before we get to my wham, bam packing methods, consider your version of….

The Box Of All Things

- Two rolls or more of toilet paper. For its intended use plus cleaning and more. Don't expect it to be provided for you in a new place.
- Some sort of spray and wipe surface cleaner. Some people leave things beyond icky!
- Packing tape for sticking down a multitude of things.
- Scissors, one or more pairs. There will be boxes to cut open and more.
- Tea/coffee/milk/sugar/kettle/disposable cups and spoons. People will be gagging.
- Biscuits, if you want to keep your paid or unpaid helpers happy.
- Lease documents for both old and new place. If you need to prove something you don't want to tear through 50 boxes to find the documents.
- Cleaning wipes. It's just easier. Get a large quantity.
- Dish-washing liquid. It's a multi-purpose cleaner.
- A large multipack of sponges/cloths. Other people's filth should be chucked and not

smeared over surfaces many times.
- Germ-killing spray. Sometimes things are…less than fresh.
- At least three pairs of rubber gloves. If you don't want to touch it, no one else does either.
- Large, strong bin bags. Lots of them!
- A sharpie or other marker. It's always good to be prepared.

One More Night
You'll also need a personal care box that is last to leave but first on the scene. It will be your survival kit for a few days. Less, if you manage a moving miracle!
- Any regular skincare
- Regular medications plus Panadol and bandaids
- Can't live without it makeup
- Deodorant
- A clean set of clothes, including shoes and underwear
- Toothbrush and paste
- Body wash
- Perfume
- A handbag with keys, wallet and ID
- Towel

Silicon Spaghetti
As I'm packing I try to keep cords with the items they fit, such as stereos and TVs. But I separate all the double adapters, extension cords and power boards. You'll need them ASAP at the new place and you'll never find them if they are not together. I polled some friends and we all agree that no matter how many we have, there are never enough double adapters, extension cords and power boards. If you can spare the cash, buying a couple of each of those items is always handy. We also agreed we like to have music at the new place to unpack to but we still like having music at the old place when we clean. Keep that in mind as you get things ready to go.

SECRETS OF THE SERIAL MOVER
I've mentioned that I've moved a lot and so have my friends. Here are our short cuts to getting it done. They won't work in every moving situation but for short distance moves (less than an hour by car between old place and new) and if you have the muscle, they're ace!

Switching Kitchens: Take the full kitchen drawers out of the cabinets in the old place and lay them carefully in the car. Tip the old drawers in to the drawers at the new place. Return drawers to old house.

Ice to a T: You'll have to empty your refrigerator into a cooler box, but for short distances, just tape the freezer shut and move it full.

Hefty Chests: If you have the muscle (check with professional movers, if using), leave things in drawers and tape them shut. The chest of drawers could be moved whole.

Bag and Tag: No need to pack your hanging clothes, just grab a handful of hangers and secure them together with an elastic band around the neck of the hangers. Cut a hole in the base of a large garbage bag, push the hangers through and pull the bag over the clothes. They can be thrown in a car or van and you can simply hang them at the other end and cut off the bag and elastic.

Towel Down: Use your towels and other linens to wrap artwork, lamps and other breakables. That's two birds moved with one stone.

Bedding Down: I always put clean bedding on, just a couple of days before the move. Then on moving morning, I carefully peel up the corners of the sheets and roll all the bedding up carefully and put it in a garbage bag. Then I can roll it straight on at the other end.

Your Stuff's Here, Now What?

Once all your stuff has been moved, it's not quite time for beer and pizza! It's Bed and Breakfast time. If you haven't already, set up a coffee station in the kitchen from your 'Box of All Things'. Get your bed constructed and made. Trust me, you'll appreciate being able to drop into bed at the end of the day. Set up your One More Night stuff in the bathroom and then it's beer and pizza time.

If you can, get your clothes unpacked and then the bathroom and then the kitchen. More power to you if you can accomplish this on moving day. These are the biggest needs in general but it makes life functional especially if you have to work on Monday. If you are working, try to unpack a box or two each day after work if you can. If it is overwhelming, just focus on getting the one box done. Don't worry, you will get there!

The Aftermath

Moving is a huge life event but sadly that never really works as an excuse. Employers, neighbours and government bodies will expect you to keep up business as usual and won't give you much leeway. You'll need to make a plan for getting rid of boxes and other packing materials. Call local recycle, get a skip or make a trip to the dump. If you didn't chuck out your junk before you moved, you'll still have that to get rid of too. And you might still have the issue of cleaning the old place. Don't freak out, just follow the spring clean list. Moving is stressful but it's over now. You'll be sure to say you'll never move again but before you know it you'll be excited to do it all over again.

Things That Go Bump In The Night

If you live alone or even with others, some things will come along (usually in the middle of the night) and freak you out. From hairy spiders to a constantly bipping smoke alarms, you can be caught off guard. And if you don't know how to deal with it, who do you call to sort it out? My BFF is married with two kids. When she was a teenager she was the sort of person who would catch the most ginormous spiders in a jar and take them outside. Then, one night, she went to check on her 18-month-old son and found a huntsman spider covering his face. Since that day, spiders have given her some serious heeby jeebies. Her husband works away, so she is not beyond calling her Dad to squish a spider. When you are on your own, and facing these situations, it can be easy to freeze or panic. I polled my pals and came up with some strategies for handling the icky, the scary and the annoying.

Things To Own For The Zombie Apocalypse (or Maybe Just Mini Emergencies)
- A good quality, knock it dead spider and bug spray.
- A dust pan and brush, long handled is very handy if your bug/mouse/spider/icky tolerance is low.
- A broom or even just a broom handle.
- A step ladder.
- A working torch – with batteries. Yes, your phone does that but it's hard to keep watch of a spider and talk on the phone. Plus blackouts happen.
- A phone.
- A friend who will take 3 am phone calls.

Prevention is Better Than Cure
Burn, Baby Burn: Service your smoke and carbon dioxide alarms at least annually. If you buy or rent a new place, get acquainted with how yours works. Does it have batteries that need changing? How do you do it and how often? Keep those batteries on hand, you'll need a step ladder to change them. If you set it off while burning the toast, how do you get it to shut off? Most need a button to be poked – the broom or broom handle is helpful here.

Power Up: When you move somewhere new, find out where the power board is and how it works. Most modern places have cut-off switches and circuit breakers that only need a switch flipping to restore power but some older houses will have filaments, cartridges or other parts that need replacing if the circuit overloads. If yours needs parts, have them on hand and be familiar with how to change them.

Knock 'em Dead: It's safe to say that where I live is the land of spiders, snakes and venomous nasties. Prevent boogly wooglies from coming in, by spraying an outdoor surface spray around windows and doors - don't forget the mailbox! A quarterly application should see you fairly free of creatures.

Put A Lock On It: Where possible get new locks when you move in to a new place. Rentals can have a lot of tenants over the years, and having a new set of locks is a good safety practice. You'll have to ask the landlord for permission. This will generally be at your cost but I think it's worth it. Lock exterior gates, accesses and mailboxes too. I've suffered break ins and it's never fun at all. I'll also add that contents' or renters' insurance is one of my essential purchases – I highly recommend it.

Light Show Fantastique: Exterior lights, especially sensor lights are a girl's best friend. No more fumbling for keys in the dark and less shadows for the shady to hide in. But remember, if you don't have black-out blinds or curtains, you could be broadcasting your silhouette for all the world to see. If you are wondering what I mean, take a walk or drive at night. You can almost see into some houses. Whether you mind what the neighbourhood sees or not, at least be aware of what can be seen.

PULLING UP THOSE BIG GIRL PANTIES
Cause For Alarm: Everyone has lived in a place where the smoke alarm goes off at the slightest provocation. I lived in one house where boiling water would have it blaring. Just use your broom or broom stick to turn it off. Never disconnect it from the main power, ever.

Once You Go Black: In the event of a blackout, stay calm, grab a torch and use your phone to check the website of your local utility. They will have estimated outage times. If there is nothing there, look at the neighbourhood to see if everyone else's lights are out. If it's just you, check your power box.

Spinning a Web: If you have a spider situation, grab your spray and make sure you're in a position to exit the room. Spray like crazy, getting as close to the spider as possible, trying not to breathe the toxic fumes. Keep an eye on it, so you know where it goes. Especially important if you have pets or kids who might eat or touch it. When it seems dead, either poke it or get ready to flush. Either pick it up with a dust pan and broom or cover with toilet roll and use long handled tongs to bury it at sea.

Look What the Cat Dragged In: If your trusty pet has brought you the gift of a disembowelled creature, the dust pan and brush is the way to go. If you are grossed right out by getting close and you don't have a long-handled version, just use a broom and steady the pan with a foot. Toss it in the garbage, job done.

Life Is Stranger Than Fiction

My mum recently had a bird fly in her back door and get trapped. Two weeks later one got trapped in the communal stairway of my apartment. Mum was able to shoosh hers out but I am a bird coward and a cat lady. If you have a trapped birdy, or indeed, if you find an injured bit of wildlife, google your local wildlife rescue.

If you come across a spider you know to be dangerous, always exercise caution. A heavy book is a good alternative to my other method.

We once had a brown snake in our yard (yeah, the country is full of things that can kill you) and that's more than a little scary. This is where you leave it alone, shut your doors and windows and call wildlife rescue. This goes for lizards too, in the hottest part of summer, my BFF's sister had one run in the door and curl up in the dog's water dish! They actually keep reptiles, so they were cool with it but I'd call wildlife rescue.

Fixing Up Accidents and Incidents

It really pays to have a well-stocked first aid kit. Colds, headaches, hangovers, minor scrapes and burns are bound to happen occasionally. I have been ever so grateful for my first aid kit when incidents and accidents occurred. Stock up your first aid kit now and be grateful later. The items on this list should be available over the counter at a pharmacy. Talk to the pharmacist about what you are buying, they will tell you when and how to use the items. If you take other medications or have allergies, be sure to let them know when seeking advice. Follow the directions on the package and any advice given by a doctor or pharmacist. Exceeding the recommended dosage or combining medicines can be dangerous, so if you are unsure, ask a doctor, pharmacist, or 24-hour health advice line. It goes without saying that all of the things listed (plus any other chemicals or medicines) should be kept out of reach of children and pets. Preferably, up high and locked. You'll want to go through your kit every 6–12 months, replacing used or expired items. Always dispose of medications safely, if you are unsure how to do that, speak to your local pharmacy for advice.

Things For the First Aid Cupboard

For Pain, Headaches and Fevers:
- Aspirin
- Ibuprofen
- Paracetamol
- Thermometer

For Congestion, Colds, and Coughs:
- Cough medicine
- Decongestant
- Throat lozenges
-

For Allergies and Itching:
- Antihistamine
- Hydrocortisone cream
- Calamine lotion
- Eye drops

For Digestive Issues:
- Antacids
- Antidiarrheal treatment
- Laxatives
- Hydra lite powder or similar body salt replacement

For Cuts and Burns:
- Sterile gauze, bandages, band aids/sticking plasters and medical tape
- Antiseptic, for wound cleaning
- Antibiotic ointment, for preventing infections from wounds
- Spray, for stings and bites
- Aloe vera gel

WHAT TO DO WHEN THINGS GO WRONG

In an emergency, the best course of action is to seek help. If someone is bleeding badly, may have a broken bone, is having a severe allergic reaction, loses consciousness or is having difficulty breathing, or stops breathing – call an ambulance. Never hesitate to seek advice or to visit a doctor if you are unsure of how to proceed. For less severe concerns such as colds and flu, head to a doctor if you are no better after 48 hours.

Knowing what do in an emergency or mini emergency can make all the difference to the outcome. If you have called an ambulance, the operator will tell you what to do while you wait. But maybe you've had a kitchen mishap, such as a cut or small burn, or you stepped on the cat's tail and twisted your ankle. As always, if you think a doctor is required, go see one. Err on the side of caution but if you decide to wait and things are no better after 48hrs, it's doctor time.

Small Cuts and Grazes

Hold a cut or graze under cool running water or pour clean water over it from a cup. Use soap to gently clean the wound. It will sting but nowhere near as much as oozing infection will. You don't need to use stronger cleaning solution or disinfectants. Smaller cuts and abrasions usually stop bleeding on their own. A cut to the head or hand may bleed more because those areas have a lot of blood vessels. Stop the bleeding by carefully applying firm, direct pressure using a clean cloth or gauze. Continue to hold the pressure steadily. Don't lift up the cloth or gauze to check on the wound, as you could cause the wound to start bleeding again. If blood seeps through the dressing, just put more on top and keep applying pressure. If you can, help slow the bleeding by raising the affected area. If the cut spurts blood or if it doesn't stop bleeding after 5 minutes, get emergency medical help right away.

Minor Burns

If possible, remove jewellery and clothing from around the injured area. If the burn is very painful, it is probably superficial. You must act quickly to reduce further injury to the skin. Immediately cool the area under cold running water until the skin returns to normal temperature (at least 20–30 minutes). Don't use iced water as this can make things worse. Cover the burn with clean, sterile (if possible), non-stick material. DO NOT use adhesive dressings, apply fat, ointment or lotions, break a blister or touch a burn.

If a burn has any of the following features, treat it as a severe burn and get immediate medical help.

- Redness that involves major joints or the face, hands, feet, genitals or buttocks.
- Blistering or very red blotchy skin that covers an area larger than a small coin.
- Blackened, or dry, white areas.
- If the burn is larger than a small coin, go to the emergency department of your local hospital.

Sunburn

There is no cure for sunburn, except time and patience. But these things might make you feel better!

- Drink plenty of water; spending time in the sun can lead to dehydration as well as sunburn.
- Gently apply cool or cold compresses or bathe the area in cool water.
- Avoid using soap as this may irritate your skin.
- Speak to a pharmacist about products that help soothe sunburn. Choose spray-on solutions rather than creams that require rubbing in.
- Do not apply butter to sunburnt skin. This is an old wives' tale. Don't pop blisters.
- Consider covering itchy blisters with a wound dressing to reduce the risk of infection.
- If your skin is not too painful, apply moisturiser. This won't stop the burnt skin from peeling off, but it will help boost the moisture content of the skin beneath.
- Take over-the-counter pain relief medication, if necessary.
- Keep out of the sun until your skin has completely healed.

See a doctor or seek treatment from the nearest hospital emergency department if you experience:
- Severe sunburn with extensive blistering and pain.
- Sunburn over a large area of skin.
- Headache.
- Nausea and vomiting.
- Fever.
- Dizziness or altered states of consciousness.

Sprains and Strains, Bruises and Bumps

Sprains and strains are soft tissue injuries that may be sudden (acute) or get worse gradually (chronic). They can take between two and 12 weeks to heal, depending on the injury, initial and ongoing treatment and the age and general health of the person. Treat sprains, strains, bumps and bruises by following these steps in order:

- Stop your activity.
- Rest the injured area.
- Apply ice packs every two hours for 15 minutes and separated from the skin by a damp towel.
- Compress or bandage the injured site firmly, extending the wrapping from below to above.
- Elevate the injured area above heart height whenever practical.
- Avoid exercise, heat, alcohol and massage, which can exacerbate swelling.
- If symptoms get worse in the first 24 hours, or things feel very wrong after 48 hours, see your doctor for further medical investigation.

WHO YOU GONNA CALL?

I know that Google will provide any number at the tap of a few buttons but having a few emergency numbers on the refrigerator (or pin board or wherever) is super helpful. It might just save time and the situation. If you are sending a housemate off in an ambulance, you probably want to let their family know and the ambulance staff will need to know of any allergies or regular medications the patient takes. We all react to emergencies differently and you'll be surprised at what you might forget in the heat of the moment. I suggest the following:

- Who you would like contacted in an emergency (such as parents or sibling), even if you live alone.
- The names and contact details of people that housemates would like to be contacted in the event of an emergency.
- A list of allergies and/or regular medications for everyone in the house. Health insurance information for everyone in the house.
- Local doctor.
- Local emergency doctor/practice/service.
- 24-hour health helpline.
- 24-hour poisons information line.
- Ambulance/Fire/Police attendance.

Big Shopping and Budget Basics

Ah money, it's never a problem if you have enough! I'm not going to bore you with spreadsheets and numbers but there are a few finance tips and things to think about that can help you fit everything into your budget. Knowledge is power and knowing where your cash is at is a big part of personal power.

A LITTLE OF COLUMN A AND A LITTLE OF COLUMN B

It's really important that you include ALL your expenses in your budget. That means nights out, gifts for friends and all the beauty stuff too. Here's some costs you need to think about including:

Column A – Pay these first

- Rent/mortgage.
- Utilities – water, power, gas.
- Technology – phones (mobile and fixed), internet connection.
- Credit cards and other debts.
- Vehicle – registration, insurance, maintenance, road tolls and work-related parking.
- Food.
- Insurance – health, renters/contents.
- Emergency savings – 10 per cent of your income is ideal.
- Other household costs such as council rates or taxes.
- Educational costs – course fees, books, materials.

Column B – Other things you should include, especially things that are regular that you wouldn't want to have to go without:

- Nights out and entertainment.
- New clothes, shoes and accessories.
- Skincare and makeup.
- Hairdressing.
- Beauty services – nails, spray tans, facials, lash extensions.
- Gifts and celebrations.
- Gym memberships and fitness costs.
- Hobbies – scrapbooking, sewing, skydiving, whatever you like to get up to.

DIVIDE AND CONQUER

So now that you know what your expenses are, you need to break it down so that each expense is in the same period. That is weekly, fortnightly, monthly, quarterly. You probably want to work things out to your pay period, so if you get paid fortnightly, your expenses are broken down to fortnightly amounts. Many people get this wrong and it can cause you hassle and the expense of late fees. A month is rarely exactly four weeks. It's hard to explain but easy to show.

The Bill Comes	And you'd like it in	Take the amount of the bill and
Weekly	Fortnightly	Times by 52, then divide by 26
	Monthly	Times by 52, then divide by 12
	Quarterly	Times by 52, then divide by 4
Fortnightly	Weekly	Times by 26, then divide by 52
	Monthly	Times by 26, then divide by 12
	Quarterly	Times by 26, then divide by 4
Monthly	Weekly	Times by 12, then divide by 52
	Fortnightly	Times by 12, then divide by 26
	Quarterly	Times by 12, then divide by 4
Quarterly	Weekly	Times by 4, then divide by 52
	Fortnightly	Times by 4, then divide by 26
	Monthly	Times by 4, then divide by 12

Maybe you looked at the table and thought, 'I don't get why you have to do it that way?' A friend of mine got a car loan. It had fortnightly repayments of let's say $150. Or for an annual figure, according to my chart, we multiply the amount by 26 and get $3,900. My friend decided to pay monthly and so was paying $300 per calendar month. She was shocked to find that she was $300 in arrears at the end of the year! Remember, I said that not every month had an even four week? By just paying the fortnightly amount twice per month only 24 payments were made. But there are 26 fortnights in a year. It's a little mind bending when you think about it and I spent plenty of years in finance explaining it. Even if you don't fully get it, just use the table above to change things from one time period to another and you should be fine. It doesn't matter if you are working in dollars, pounds, euros, rupees, yen, baht or any currency, the principles are the same. If you are unsure, always contact the service provider and ask them to give you a hand.

CRUNCHING THE NUMBERS

Energy or utility bills are likely to fluctuate between seasons, so be sure to keep that in mind. As I mentioned when chatting about roommates, be aware of your financial obligations with bills, in your own or in joint names. I have made every classic financial mistake, sometimes more than once. It's a little laughable that I ended up working in finance but once I understood how money worked I never screwed up again. Have some hints and tips from my experiences.

Fees and Charges: Talk to your bank and make sure you have the right accounts for the way you use yours. Don't get pinged for needless fees. Always have some sort of savings account to squirrel cash away.

Add It Up: Even $10 per pay can make a small cushion of savings. Do whatever you can do.

Don't Stick Your Head In the Sand: Do not ignore calls and mail. Ignorance is no defence and it won't wash legally.

Beg For Small Mercies: Negotiate with creditors as soon as possible. If you cannot meet a commitment, try to make an agreement but you must be able to stick to it.

Ask for Help: No not a loan, help. If you are in over your head, talk to someone who can help you make a plan to go forward with.

Be Wary of Credit: Understand the fine print, measure the real (with interest) costs. You know, in your heart, if you trust yourself. If you don't trust, don't do it.

She Lives So Fine. It's so easy to think that others are cashed up. You watch them living the good life, wearing their designer wardrobe and driving their fancy car. I want you to know that I have seen those people and been shocked to see a home loan of nearly a million dollars, his and hers personal loans and credit card debt the price of a small flat. They are sinking and drowning but they'll look good doing it. After the things I've seen, for me, flashy equals debt, not money. Please don't join their ranks.

BUYING UP BIG

So, you need to buy a big ticket item – a refrigerator, washer, dryer. Or maybe you need something less major such as a camera, TV or laptop. Refrigerators, washers and dryers are all long-term commitments, the other things less so. Either way you want to buy the best thing at the best price. Most of the time, you'll have time to linger over reviews and get a sense of what you want and need but sometimes, it's a right now, no time to think deal. I've had some funny moments with big appliances. I took my Gran's refrigerator when she went into the nursing home. It was quite new and I thought I'd have it for ages. Two years later, Gran passed away and to be perfectly honest, checking the temperature of my refrigerator was miles from my mind. When I thudded back to reality, I realised my refrigerator died on the same day as she did. All my food needed chucking but more urgently I needed a new refrigerator quickly! I measured the space where the new refrigerator would sit in my flat and I knew the one I wanted would fit. But imagine my surprise when they came to deliver it and couldn't get it up the narrow stairway outside my apartment!? To make sure you don't make that mistake, or others, here's a handy guide to getting the big buys right.

Rave Reviews: There are a world of online reviews, just waiting for you, for almost any product. Check them out before you buy but remember that most people who are simply happy with a product will probably not bother to post. People with bad experiences are much more likely to shout from the roof tops.

Measure Twice: Know how big the space for your appliance is and also any hallways, stairwells, door frames it will have to go through to get there.

Muscling In: How will you get it home? Does it come with delivery? Can a friend help?

Know What You Need: What features are truly important? What can you do without?

Talk Up A Bargain. You should always price check the item you want and negotiate the best deal you can. Never feel bad about it. I once talked a $600 vacuum down to $385. Never be rude, just calmly negotiate.

Healthy Suspicion: Treat all interest-free, pay nothing now, rent-to-own and in-house finance with suspicion. Don't let want get in the way. If you are not sure, ask someone you trust to look over it.

Sometimes Second Wins: If cash is tight, consider scratch'n'dent, floor models, outlet malls and second hand. I have had many bargains this way and most often, no one will tell the difference.

A Final Word

I'm going to believe that as you read, you got things done. Which means you will now need to put your feet up and relax as you deserve. Trust me there, are no weird platitudes or advice, just domestic life wisdom! However, here is my last word of advice – when life give you lemons, you could – clean your kettle or your work surfaces. Or maybe just make this cocktail…

THE LEMON DROP
45 ml (1½ fl oz) vodka
30 ml (1 fl oz) lemon juice
1 teaspoon simple syrup
Lemon twist, to decorate

1. Pour the liquid ingredients into a cocktail shaker with ice cubes and shake well.
2. Strain into a chilled cocktail glass.
3. Decorate with the lemon twist and ENJOY.
4. Even if everything is not completely cleaned and decorated I hope that now your home makes you simply squeak with joy! I hope you feel armed, empowered and confident for any situation that arises. I want you to feel wonderful about where you live because you really deserve that… So join me and sit back, sip a cocktail and go on living your life with flair!

To Make Simple Syrup

200 g (7 oz/1 cup) white (granulated) sugar
250 ml (8 fl oz/1 cup) water

1. Bring to a boil and cook until sugar is dissolved. Allow to cool before using in cocktails. Store the remainder in a sealed glass container in the refrigerator for up to 3 months.

I believe in your mad, crazy, amazing skills.

Sarah xxxx